THE CASE OF STEPHEN DOWNING

The Worst Miscarriage of Justice in British History

STEPHEN DOWNING

Foreword by former police intelligence officer Chris Clark

PEN & SWORD
TRUE CRIME

First published in Great Britain in 2019 by
PEN AND SWORD TRUE CRIME
an imprint of
Pen and Sword Books Ltd
47 Church Street
Barnsley
South Yorkshire S70 2AS

ISBN 978 1 52674 202 5

Printed and bound in the UK
by TJ International, Padstow, Cornwall, PL28 8RW

Typeset in Times New Roman 11.5/14 by
Aura Technology and Software Services, India

Pen & Sword Books Ltd incorporates the imprints of Pen & Sword
Archaeology, Atlas, Aviation, Battleground, Discovery,
Family History, History, Maritime, Military, Naval, Politics, Railways,
Select, Social History, Transport, True Crime, Claymore Press,
Frontline Books, Leo Cooper, Praetorian Press, Remember When,
Seaforth Publishing and Wharncliffe.

For a complete list of Pen and Sword titles please contact
Pen and Sword Books Limited
47 Church Street, Barnsley, South Yorkshire, S70 2AS, England
E-mail: enquiries@pen-and-sword.co.uk
Website: www.pen-and-sword.co.uk

THE CASE OF STEPHEN DOWNING

Contents

Foreword

Wendy Sewell, a 32-year-old married legal secretary, worked for the Forestry Commission at Catcliffe House, Church Street in Bakewell, Derbyshire. At about 12.20 pm on Wednesday, 12 September 1973 John Osmaston, the commission's district officer, was on the telephone in his office when Wendy handed him a note to say that she was going out for a breath of fresh air. Later, Osmaston would say that just prior to this, he heard a man's voice in Wendy's office, which he described as shrill, high pitched and agitated. Several people saw Wendy walking along Butts Road and around Bakewell Cemetery. A passerby, Charles Carman, saw her enter the cemetery through Burton Edge, and walk along the back path. The time was 12.50 pm and his was the last recorded sighting of her before she was attacked. She was beaten round the head with the handle of a pickaxe, a violent assault which appeared to be sexually motivated as her trousers, pants, plimsolls and parts of her bra had been removed. She died from her injuries in Chesterfield Royal Hospital two days later.

In the meantime, Wilfred Walker, the cemetery attendant who lived in the lodge by the main gate, saw the cemetery's 17-year-old groundskeeper, Stephen Downing, walk out of the gates with a fizzy pop bottle under his arm. Although nothing struck him as unusual about the young man's clothes or demeanour, he noticed that when Downing walked back through the gates a few minutes later, he no longer had the bottle. While Downing had been away, two council cemetery workmen, Eric Fox and Fred Hawksworth, had entered the cemetery in order to go to the store. A few minutes later Downing came across the unconscious and bloodied body of Wendy Sewell and tried to render first aid before going to the lodge to get Walker, who went with him to the scene of the attack.

Downing told police that he had found Wendy Sewell lying on the ground, covered in blood, and that her blood got on his clothes when she shook her head. Despite having learning difficulties and a reading age of 11, he was arrested, questioned for eight hours without a solicitor present and signed a confession.

Downing's trial took place between 13 and 15 February 1974 at Nottingham Crown Court before Mr Justice Nield and a jury. He pleaded not guilty. Forensic scientist Norman Lee gave evidence and said the blood found on the accused could only have been present if he had been responsible for the assault. Lee described this evidence as 'a textbook example...which might be expected on the clothing of the assailant.' After reaching a unanimous verdict, the jury found Downing guilty of murder and he was sentenced to be detained indefinitely, with a stipulation that he should serve a minimum of seventeen years.

There are three files held at The National Archives in Kew on the 1973 murder of Wendy Sewell. Two of these, J 188/63 and DPP 2/5332, are closed until 2069 and 2070 respectively. One file, J82/3322, is an open document and has been since 1 January 2005 and it is from this file that I have taken extracts:

> 'In the Nottingham Crown Court Case Number: 1128/B1/74 on 13 February 1974 before the Honourable Mr Justice Nield Regina –V– Stephen Leslie Downing charged with the murder of Wendy Sewell on the 14th day of September 1973. For the Prosecution Mr P Bennett QC and Mr K Matthewman and for the Defence Mr D Barker QC and Mr J Warren. From the Shorthand notes of J L Harpham Ltd Official Shorthand Writers, 55 Queen Street, Sheffield S1 2DX.

> 'Clerk: "Are you Stephen Leslie Downing?"
> Downing: "Yes."
> Clerk: "Stephen Leslie Downing you are charged in this indictment with murder. The particulars of the offence are that you on the 14th day of September 1973 in the County of Derby, murdered Wendy Sewell. Now, how say you to this charge, are you guilty or not guilty?"
> Downing: "Not Guilty."'

Mr Bennett opened the case on behalf of the prosecution and the statement from pathologist Dr Alan Usher was among those read out.

FOREWORD

The following day Mr Barker opened the case on behalf of the defence. On 15 February the judge summed up and the jury retired at 11.28 am to consider the case. At 12.28 pm, they came back with a unanimous verdict of guilty. Mr Justice Nield concluded with the words:

> 'Well you have been found guilty on the clearest evidence of this very serious offence. The court has but one sentence in its power to pass and that is you will be detained during Her Majesty's pleasure. Put him down please.'

But Downing had a lifeline. A witness was found who said she saw Stephen Downing leaving the cemetery at the same time as she saw Wendy Sewell alive and unharmed. Downing applied for leave to appeal on the grounds he had a new witness who saw Wendy Sewell walking towards the back of the consecrated chapel. In the Court of Appeal at the Royal Courts of Justice on Friday, 25 October 1974, Lord Justice Orr, Mr Justice Shaw and Mr Justice Boreham heard the appeal in Regina –v– Stephen Leslie Downing but the witness evidence was deemed to be unreliable and the appeal was denied.

Caught in an innocent prisoner's dilemma, Stephen Downing was unable to be paroled as he did not admit to the crime. He was classified as being 'in denial of murder' and therefore ineligible for parole under English law. Downing would continue to deny the murder so his family attempted to get support for a retrial. In 1994, they wrote to the local newspaper, the *Matlock Mercury* and the editor, Don Hale, took up the case and ran a campaign. As a result of this – and Downing's persistent protestations of innocence – the case was referred to the Criminal Cases Review Commission in 1997.

Stephen Downing was released on appeal in 2001 after twenty-seven years in prison. The following year, on 15 January 2002, the Court of Appeal overturned his conviction, finding it to be unsafe. The case is thought to be the longest miscarriage of justice in British legal history and attracted worldwide media attention. During the second appeal held on 15 January 2002, the Court of Appeal accepted many of the reasons that were put forward by Don Hale and others for believing the conviction was unsafe. Julian Bevan QC accepted two arguments put forward by the defence. The first was that Downing's confession should not have been allowed to go before a jury. Not only had Downing been questioned for eight hours, during which the police shook him and pulled his hair to keep him awake, he wasn't formally cautioned that what he said may be used in evidence against him, and he wasn't given a solicitor. The Crown also agreed with the defence that more recent knowledge of blood-spatter patterns meant the prosecution's claim that the blood could only have been found on the clothes of the attacker was questionable.

The Right Honourable Lord Justice Pill said that the Court of Appeal did not have to consider whether Downing was innocent but whether the original conviction was fair. 'The question for [the Court of Appeal's] consideration is whether the conviction is safe and not whether the accused is guilty,' he said. What the defence proved was that there was reasonable doubt about the 'reliability of the confessions made in 1973'. His Lordship concluded: 'The court cannot be sure the confessions are reliable. It follows that the conviction is unsafe. The conviction is quashed.'

Following the successful appeal, Hale, with Hamish McGregor and Marika Huns wrote a book, *Town Without Pity: The Fight to Clear Stephen Downing of the Bakewell Murder.*

In May 2013 I looked at the online information about Wendy Sewell's attack and murder and realized it was similar to the method used by Peter Sutcliffe, albeit using a pickaxe handle instead of a hammer. Sutcliffe was convicted of murdering thirteen women in the mid to late 1970s and is better known as the notorious Yorkshire Ripper. On 10 July 2013, I made a Freedom of Information (FOI) request of Derbyshire Constabulary asking for the pathology report on Wendy Sewell and witness statements from those who found her, including Stephen Downing. Two weeks later I received the following extracted reply from the FOI officer:

> 'I have today decided not to disclose the located information to you as I am claiming exemptions under Section 30(1)(a) (b)(c) - Investigations and proceedings conducted by public authorities and Section 40(2) - Personal information of the Freedom of Information Act 2000; the rationales for which are shown below. Therefore please accept this letter as a formal refusal of your request.... Wendy Sewell's body was found shortly after 12.50 p.m. on 12 September 1973 in Bakewell Cemetery having been struck a number of times

to the head causing severe head injuries. Wendy was taken to the Chesterfield Royal Hospital where she died from the injuries on 14 September 1973.

'Stephen Downing, a 17 year old grounds man who has been working in the cemetery raised the alarm prior to being taken to Bakewell Police Station where he was questioned for several hours about the incident. During this questioning Stephen confessed to attacking Wendy. Following Wendy's death Stephen was charged with her murder and pleaded not guilty at this trial which took place at Nottingham Crown Court between 13 and 15 February 1974. Stephen was found guilty and sentenced to be detained at Her Majesty's Pleasure.

'Stephen applied for an extension of time within which to apply for leave to appeal and to call a new witness. The Court refused leave to appeal against conviction. The case was referred to the Criminal Cases Review Commission in 1997 who found grounds to refer it back to the Court of Appeal. On 15 January 2002 the Court of Appeal granted the appeal quashing the conviction.

'Following the Court of Appeal, the Chief Constable (David Coleman) decided that the circumstances of the original offence should be thoroughly re-investigated. This reinvestigation took 6 months from its commencement date to October 2002 following which an advice file was subsequently submitted to the Crown Prosecution Service. The police are not looking for any other person for the murder of Wendy Sewell and all possible lines of enquiry have been exhausted. Subsequently the case is now closed unless any substantial new evidence comes to light.'

In October 2013, I purchased a copy of *Town Without Pity*. Having read it, I was of the opinion that Stephen Downing was innocent of the attack on Mrs Sewell and just happened to be in the wrong place at the wrong time. A month later, I made contact with Downing's mother Juanita and sister Christine, known as Chrissie. I asked Chrissie if the family had a copy of the pathologist's report and on 2 December 2013 she emailed it to me. A day later, I replied to say that, on reading, it was quite clear to me that Wendy Sewell was attacked from behind with a garrotte looped over her neck, which when tightened would cause asphyxia and partial lack of consciousness before being struck with the pickaxe handle and being kicked. I drew her attention to the section headed 'larynx' which said 'massive ecchymoses in the mucus membrane below the level of the false vocal cords'. In layman's terms this means a big bruise on the Adam's apple, which I believe was caused by a knot. Under the section 'cervical muscles' it said 'some bruising of the deep cervical muscles'. Simply put this means the back of the neck had been squeezed, which would be expected when using a garrotte by applying a tourniquet twist. Under 'trachea and air passages' it said 'congested with numerous petechiae'. This means the air passages had filled with frothy mucus and it is a characteristic finding of asphyxiation, which results from the haemorrhage of end capillaries as blood is pumped through dead cells. Later it says 'Sections of lung showed some congestion and in places frank haemorrhage in the alveoli; the air passages were full of basophilic mucus.'

I found it incredible that despite three senior detectives being present at the mortuary at the time of the post-mortem examination being carried out by the pathologist, no mention was made of these findings at the trial, the appeal or during Operation Noble in 2002, when police reinvestigated the case after Downing's sentence was quashed.

Peter Sutcliffe used a knotted length of rope on his last three victims as well as a hammer for two murders and one attempted murder in 1980. He also kicked or stamped on some of his victims. When he was eventually searched after his arrest on 2 January 1981, he was found with a length of rope on him and had tried to dispose of a hammer and knife. Wendy Sewell was stripped in a similar way to many of his victims in a prelude to what I believe to be a stabbing and a sexual assault, but the assailant was disturbed by Stephen Downing coming back. Shortly after, she was dragged by her left arm and leg face down to where Stephen found and tended her. I believe the attacker then ran into Catcliff Wood and into Park Road and then via the footpath in Park Road to the 'kissing gate' and Butts Road. I believe that person was Peter Sutcliffe, the Yorkshire Ripper.

Chris Clark, former police intelligence officer and co-author with Tim Tate of *Yorkshire Ripper: The Secret Murders*.

Introduction

The Telegraph 11 Feb 2001. Daniel Foggo writes:

'Stephen Downing, who spent 27 years in prison on a murder charge which is now certain to be quashed, has described how he was repeatedly attacked by other prisoners. Stephen Downing: "I even contemplated ending it myself at times." Mr Downing, 44, released on bail last week, says he was raped, stabbed, beaten up and twice scalded with boiling water because he was wrongly believed to be a sex offender. In fact, although he was jailed for the murder of Wendy Sewell, an autopsy showed that she was not sexually assaulted, even though she was discovered with her lower clothing missing.

'In attempting to win his freedom, Downing says he was subjected to further intimidation, this time at the hands of the prison authorities. When Don Hale, his local newspaper editor in Matlock, Derbyshire, made clear his intention to champion the cause in 1995, Mr Downing was moved from a "cushy prison" in Dorchester, Dorset, to the "Colditz-like" inhospitality of HMP Dartmoor.

'There he was placed in a cold cell and pressurised into admitting his "guilt" by prison officers.

'He said: "My Dartmoor cell had a cracked window and was so cold I used to wear a T-shirt, shirt, sweatshirt, denim jacket and donkey jacket to bed, with a balaclava and socks on my hands for mittens. The prison authorities put a lot of pressure on me to confess to the murder over the years. Nothing was said officially but officers told me I would die in prison unless I confessed. They just could not admit that there could be innocent men inside. But I knew I had no chance of ever clearing my name if I confessed – although by insisting my innocence I served more than 10 years longer than my tariff."

'Officials also tried to force him to undertake a rehabilitation course for sex offenders, refusing to hear his protestations that it did not apply to him. When eventually they made him attend the sessions he was thrown out because he would not declare himself to have committed a sex crime. Mr Downing was moved again and again as he continued to protest his innocence. He was incarcerated in some of Britain's most horrific institutions, including "grisly" Risley, the remand centre with a particularly high suicide rate. Mr Downing said: "I even contemplated ending it myself at times when I was very down in the early stages during the very dark days." Today he can talk of his early years in jail only with great difficulty. "It happened early on and it was really brutal. I was just a young lad then and easy prey for others." He became a target for the prison bullies because he had signed a confession, written for him by the Derbyshire detectives investigating the murder of Mrs Sewell, stating that he had sexually attacked 32-year-old Mrs Sewell and then murdered her.

'Although a post-mortem examination found no evidence of any sexual assault and Mr Downing subsequently consistently denied attacking or killing her, it was this confession and the method by which the police extracted it that will almost certainly lead to the Court of Appeal to rule his conviction unsafe when a full hearing is convened in May. The detectives had failed to caution Mr Downing, who was almost illiterate and allegedly had a mental age of 11, sufficiently beforehand or give him access to a solicitor.

'Describing how he was skewered through the hand with a fork by another inmate, he said: "I have been attacked, insulted, beaten up and abused." A row in a dinner queue had become heated and he had his food kicked to the floor by the man, who then stabbed him. On other occasions he had scalding water thrown at him and was shown a vat of bubbling liquid into which he was told sex offenders were immersed as part of their "initiation" into the prison system. He said: "I was under attack from those who chose to call me a nonce [sex offender] but I ignored them, which I am sure annoyed them."

'A quietly spoken, shy man, he is given to understatement. He said: "I've had to suffer my share. Although I tried not to let it show on the surface, inside myself was a different story." His battle for freedom has been made more protracted by his refusal to concede having had any part in her death: prisoners cannot be paroled unless they accept their crime and show repentance. Mr Downing wants to try to rebuild his life by pursuing a career in catering, going to college or even starting a business once his impending civil damages claim has worked its way through the courts.'

This newspaper report is full of errors. I have never been raped, stabbed or scalded by anyone at any time. I was never 'shown a vat of bubbling liquid' and I have never been suicidal. Yes, I've been called names, just like many others in prison, but this was mainly by sex offenders who were looking to divert attention from themselves.

Chapter 1

Birth and Early Life

I was born on Sunday, 4 March 1956 at home. My mother Juanita, known to everyone as Nita, had been adopted at the age of 3 and brought up in the Bowring Park district of Huyton-with-Roby in Liverpool. She had married my father, Ray, a young RAF man, in 1954 and we lived at 50 Burton Edge in Bakewell, Derbyshire, sharing the house with my grandparents on my father's side until they were allocated a council house. Three years later to the day, on Wednesday, 4 March 1959 my sister Christine – Chrissie to everyone – was born in our new family home at 16 Holywell Flats in Bakewell.

Mum and Dad's wedding 1954.

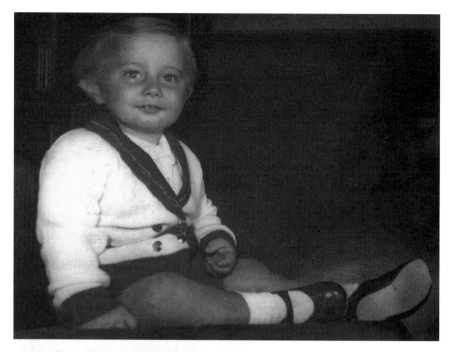

Above: Me aged two.

Left: Me with Dad's cousin Dora Harbottle.

Right: My sister Chrissie
and me with Grandma Dora
(Dad's mother).

Below: Family photo April 1961.

Mum and Dad with Chrissie 1962.

Following the loss of my grandfather, Percy, a short while after my sister's birth, my grandmother, Dora, moved into 11 Holywell Flats, having exchanged with her niece and husband. However, as we got older, my mother struggled to get the pram up and down the stone steps to the upstairs flat, so we did a swap with my grandmother and we moved into number 11.

We had many happy years at the flat, which was located on a very quiet estate, with perhaps no more than three or four people owning a car. We bought a second hand Austin A40 so my father could get to work quicker as he had joined the ambulance service. In those days it really was 'swoop and scoop' and get them to the nearest hospital as quick as the ambulance would allow.

As we grew older it was no longer acceptable for us to share a bedroom so our parents applied for a transfer and in 1967, when I was 11 and Chrissie was 8, we moved into the house my sister still calls home. My mother didn't like the house from the start but beggars can't be choosers with council homes so she was stuck with it. The first thing on the to-do list was put light bulbs in the rooms as the previous tenant had taken them with her. My mother insisted on decorating the kitchen orange and white, which I guess was to brighten the place up. Like most households at that time, the kitchen was the hub of the home and where friends would congregate when they called round for a cup of tea.

Me and Chrissie with our Austin A40 circa 1964.

Scarborough summer 1960: Dad, me, Grandma Eva (Mum's mother), Chrissie and Mum.

Money was tight and my parents were careful spenders. The most extravagant purchase was the car. Holidays were few and far between and when we did go away, it would be a week in Scarborough where my grandmother's sister had a bed and breakfast or a week in Liverpool with my mother's parents. One of my dad's work colleagues had a small caravan in Llandudno, North Wales, and we enjoyed a week there. It wasn't until later, when my father left the ambulance service and started work as a coach driver, that we had several holidays in Cliftonville in Margate on the Kent coast. My last trip was in August 1973, just a few weeks before my arrest.

I was a year late starting Bakewell Infant School because I had bronchitis and pleurisy. It was so bad that the doctor wouldn't allow me to be moved to hospital as he didn't think I'd survive the journey. Instead, a bed was made up in the living room from two armchairs tied together. It wasn't the best of setups but I enjoyed being there. My mother and grandmother would sit up alternate nights to watch over me and as I didn't sleep well, I'd sit up and chat with them as they read stories to me. Once I started school, I found it hard to make friends as my peers were already settled and I had to try and fit in.

My first day at school.

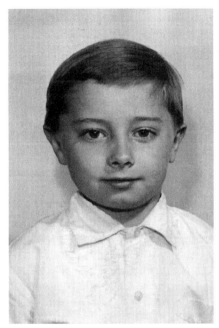 

Above left: School photo circa 1962.

Above right: School photo circa 1964.

Below: Me, aged seven with Mum, Dad and Chrissie.

A family photo to treasure 1964.

Eventually I did make friends and they would stay with me as I progressed through Bakewell Methodist Junior School and Bath Street Boys' School, which was Church of England. Most of us lived within a minute or two of each other and would meet up in the evening after school and at weekends. I left school aged 15 on a Friday morning after an assembly full of hymns and a lecture by Headmaster Harry Schofield, who was also the local magistrate. I sat at the front with the other leavers, facing the crowd of younger pupils. Even though I was leaving school with no qualifications (I only excelled in Woodwork), he told everyone that we had done well and were well prepared for what lay ahead. He then shook each of us by the hand as we filed out of the hall. I had been growing my hair long but my mother had been badgering me to get it cut and that morning she

Me aged eight at Bakewell Methodist Junior School.

had thrust some money into my hand, so off I went to the barbers before meeting a mate in a nearby café where we played the pinball machines for a couple of hours before drifting home. As I walked through the door, I could have cried when my mother commented on my hair cut and told me she'd liked it long! It would be many years before my hair saw scissors again.

So now I was in the big wide world aged 15 but with a reading age of an 11-year-old. Fortunately, I found work quickly at Bloomers the Bakers, home of the mouth-watering Bloomers' Original Bakewell Pudding, which had a shop and restaurant on Matlock Street in the town centre. I loved working there. Perhaps it was my true vocation. One of my proudest moments was when a bread wheatsheaf I had designed and baked was chosen as the centrepiece of the harvest festival in the local parish church. The local vicar at the time, who I think may have been Rev Urquhart, had asked for one and Eric Bloomer, the boss, thought it was something I could do.

Despite my poor learning ability at school I had developed a mischievous sense of humour and had a keen eye for observation. One day I asked why there were only gingerbread men and never any women. Eric's son, John, suggested I make one and an example of my handiwork had many people chuckling, though John's mother-in-law was not impressed and tut-tutted when she saw it in the bakehouse. My gingerbread woman didn't go any further, which was a disappointment, not just to me but to the customers who thought she was hilarious and had already put in their orders. I had a good time at Bloomers and despite my employers taking a liking to this agreeable, simple lad from the council estate, after a year they decided to dispense with my services. I can't pretend I don't know why – I was more than often late for work.

My next job lasted just five days. I worked for a plasterer but was dismissed almost immediately and despite asking why, I was never told. I then started work at Cintride, an engineering works, where I managed to stay for five months before I was again sacked for bad timekeeping. I really didn't know what to do. I loved cars and my dream was to become a grease monkey but attempts to find work with local garages proved fruitless. I could strip a car to bits and I could have spent days rebuilding it and fault-finding along the way. I had a lot of patience for this kind of intricate work and I enjoyed making things. I loved building models and even embroidery, which was unusual for teenage boys. However, my real passions were cooking and baking, which would prove to be great assets later on in prison.

Bloomers the bakers, where I worked.

Chapter 2

Murder in the Cemetery

In September 1973 I was 17 years old, a naïve and somewhat backward young man, who lacked qualifications and was a little too trusting. I was working for the council, maintaining the grounds at Bakewell Cemetery just a few hundred yards up the road from my home. I was quite happy there and had no ambition to look for anything more fruitful. Looking back, I think I would still be there now had it not been for the life-shattering event to come. Like many teenagers I wasn't one for mornings. However, on Wednesday, 12 September 1973 I got myself off to work just on time. I'd spent the two previous days at home with a nasty cold and despite my mother's suggestion that I should take more time off to recover, I decided to go in. I enjoyed what I did and for the most part I worked alone, which I didn't mind. As long as I made the place look as nice as possible for visitors, I was left to get on with it. The only time I went anywhere with my workmates was on a Friday when we finished work an hour early and went to the town hall to collect our wages.

I arrived at the depot at 7.55 am, as we were expected to arrive five minutes before the hour to give us time to book in. Even so it would be at least 8.30 am before anyone made a move to do some work. A cup of tea and a read of the morning paper took priority over anything else, although I wasn't one for reading and used to bring my own thermos of coffee. That morning went smoothly and without incident. I'd done quite a lot of mowing the week before so today I had to trim the edges of the flower borders, which was back-breaking work.

I had run out of petrol for the mowers so before leaving the depot to head to the cemetery, I asked for a gallon to take with me. I was just leaving with the can in my hand when a colleague, Herbert Dawson, told me he was going up to the cemetery with a fellow workmate, Eric Fox, and offered me a lift. I climbed into the back of the Land Rover and as we made our way to the cemetery, they told me they were looking for an asbestos chimney cowl. The unconsecrated chapel was used to store tools and they soon found what they were looking for and were gone before I'd finished loading a wheelbarrow with the tools I needed for that day. Before I left the unconsecrated chapel I found some solid fuel and after dipping a few bits of wood in the petrol I soon had a fire burning in the pot-bellied stove in the corner. It was quite a sharp day with some mist about and even a touch of frost on the bushes and grass.

I busied myself near the bank that ran parallel to the lower road of Burton Edge. As usual I became absorbed in the job and lost track of time. Then I heard the striking of the church clock so I stopped what I was doing and took out my father's pocket watch. My watch was broken so I'd borrowed his and to keep it safe I'd wrapped it in cotton wool and put it in a pipe tobacco tin. It was 10.00 am so I gathered up the tools and took myself off to the chapel, poured a coffee from my thermos and smoked a cigarette. Five or six minutes later, I made my way back outside and finished off the area.

With that done, I began clipping the grass around some of the graves. I hadn't been there long when a woman's voice said, 'Hello, Stephen. Where have you been? I've not seen you for a couple of days.' I stopped and turned to reply. I recognized her as a local dog walker and, although I'm not sure, I think her name was Mary Hatfield. I told her I'd been off with a cold and she suggested I put a coat on. I explained that even though it was misty with a nip in the air, the work kept me warm.

As my lunch break was nearing its end and I'd finished my bottle of lemonade, I decided to nip to Evans, the nearby shop and hope I made it before they closed for their lunch break at 1.00 pm. It was just after the hour but even if they were closed, I could pop home and leave a note for my mother to get me another bottle this afternoon. I finished smoking my cigarette on the steps just outside and to the right of the unconsecrated chapel when I noticed a woman walking round the bottom section of the cemetery, home to the new plots, looking at the graves. I can't say I had ever seen her before. As there had been some desecration of the graves – flowers taken and headstones damaged – I had been keeping an eye out for strangers in the area. However, these acts of vandalism were probably caused by kids rather than young women so I stubbed out my cigarette and went back into the chapel to get my coat and pick up the empty lemonade bottle. I then made my way down the centre drive towards the main gate. As I carried on, I noticed the same woman walking along the bottom footpath, heading in the same direction as me, although she was some distance in front. I remember thinking that it had not taken her very long to cover a distance of about 150 yards, especially as she appeared to be strolling. I certainly hadn't heard her pass the unconsecrated chapel. I continued on the centre drive, fully expecting the woman to pass from behind the consecrated chapel, but she didn't. As I passed it myself I glanced to my right to see if I could catch sight of her, but she was gone. I assumed she'd turned back to walk around the cemetery again.

Drawing close to the cemetery lodge, I noticed Wilf Walker standing in the doorway behind his wife who was sitting in a deckchair. We exchanged greetings and I passed through the main gate and crossed the road. I bumped into our next-door neighbour, Peter Moran Senior, and we said hello. A few yards on, I met and spoke to Charlie Carmen who was a colleague on his way back to work after his lunch break. As I got to Evans, I noticed the shop was already closed as the blinds were down so I made my way home in order to leave my mother a note about a replacement bottle of lemonade.

On arrival, I went to the garage to change out of my dress boots – which I kept for best – and into my work boots. Normally, I would do this first thing in the morning but that day I hadn't as I didn't want to be late for work having been off for the previous two days. When I put the key in

Aerial view showing Bakewell Cemetery and our home.

the front door, it was already unlocked and my mother called to say it was open. She was taking off her coat, having just come home on the 1.00 pm bus and she offered me a drink but I declined and asked if she would buy me another Jusoda bottle when the shop opened. She agreed and offered to drop it off at my work. I counted out the money and left it on the kitchen table saying that it would be enough with the 3p return on the empty bottle. I bid her a cheery farewell and made my way back to work, stopping only to check on some baby hedgehogs in our garden, which I'd found abandoned. I didn't meet anyone on the way back.

When I got to the main gate, I noticed Wilf and his wife had gone into the lodge taking the deckchair with them. The walk had warmed me up so I took off my jacket and, with my finger through the hanging loop, tossed it over my shoulder. The cemetery was still and empty. I hadn't gone much further when I noticed something on the lower path between the headstones and walked over to see what it was. As I neared, I realized it was a person lying face down so I started running and then saw it was a woman, naked from the waist down with her jumper pulled up above her breasts, her bra visible. Clothing was scattered on the path by her feet. Instinctively, I knelt down beside her and rolled her on to her back. Her hair was soaked in blood. It was all over her face and there was a large, spreading pool of it on the ground. I put my fingers to her neck to see if I could detect a pulse but there was nothing. I placed my hand between her breasts to see if I could find a heartbeat and she began to make guttural sounds from the back of her throat. Suddenly, she rose to a sitting position and shook her head from side to side. Startled, I came to my feet and stumbled back against a headstone. Just then, I felt a sharp object in the lower part of my back and a deep, gruff, male voice said, 'Don't turn round. There are two of us and if you say anything to anyone your sister will get the same.' I froze. 'Have you found it?' he asked to which another voice replied 'Yes.' It was higher pitched than the first and could have belonged to a woman although I don't know. The sharpness left my back as whatever object used to poke me was removed and, despite being ordered not to do so, I turned briefly and caught sight of the back of a head as someone jumped over the wall into Catcliff Wood. The person appeared to be quite tall, with an athletic build, had sandy-coloured hair and was wearing a denim jacket.

Wasting no more time, I ran to the lodge and hammered on the door until it was opened seconds later by Wilf Walker. I asked if he was on the phone as I wanted to call the police. He said he wasn't and asked why. I told

Photograph taken by the scenes of crime officer.

The crime scene where Wendy Sewell was attacked.

him a woman had been injured in the cemetery. He kept saying 'Where? Show me.' I pointed to where I'd found her and we ran towards it, but as we grew closer it was obvious that she was no longer there. I was totally lost for words. 'Where is she?' asked Wilf and I pointed and said 'I don't know, she was there.' Then we walked a little further and I caught sight of her, only now she was lying across a grave. Her clothes lay scattered as before.

The grave and headstone across which Wendy Sewell's body was lying.

Amid the shock and confusion, Wilf saw two colleagues, Fred Hawksworth and Eric Fox, and beckoned them over. He told them about the injured woman and asked if one would call an ambulance and the police, which Hawksworth agreed to do. It later transpired that both men had arrived at the cemetery while I had been away at the shop and at my mother's house and had been looking for me to help them load some asbestos sheets on to the Land Rover. We hadn't been together long when Herbert Dawson drove up in the Land Rover along with another man. They stopped beside us and were told of the woman. Then Dawson drove up to the unconsecrated chapel, parked the car and both men walked down to join us. Shortly after, one of the group and I think it may have been Wilf Walker, said that the woman was getting up. I turned to look and indeed she did get to her feet and, despite being stooped over, managed to take two or three steps before falling and striking her head on the side of the headstone on Sarah Bradbury's grave. Dawson started to push his way towards her but Fox held him back saying he shouldn't get involved. Later on we learned that after making the 999 call, Hawksworth had sat down near the main gate to take a pill for his angina.

It was at least ten minutes before a police car arrived driven by PC Ball. I believe it was Dawson who informed him that a woman was injured and indicated where she was. Ball asked who had found her and I said I had. He asked me a few more questions about where I'd found her and at what time and then Dawson came over and asked if it was all right for me to help them load the Land Rover up with the asbestos sheets and PC Ball said that it was. He went to look at the woman while I went to help the others. He then went to his car and made a radio call, before coming over to ask Hawksworth, who had now rejoined us, something although I don't know what. Then he took off his jacket and put it over the injured woman.

With the Land Rover loaded we just stood there and, about fifteen minutes after Ball had made the radio call, a convoy of plain police vehicles arrived and out spilled a number of officers in suits. They headed straight for Ball and huddled together talking. After a while the party broke up and two of the suits came over to me. They identified themselves as Detective Inspector Younger and Detective Sergeant Johnson. They started with the same string of questions: Had I found her? Where was she? What time was this? etc. I answered them and they wandered off again but before long they returned and asked if I would go to the station to answer some more questions. Eager to oblige, I agreed and was escorted to a car. As the car pulled away it was forced to stop at the main gate to allow the ambulance to enter.

At the police station, I was led upstairs into a sparsely furnished room. It was quite a large room with two desks and four straight-backed chairs, like the kind you'd find in a dining room. I was invited to sit on one while Younger perched on the edge of the desk and Johnson hovered close to my left shoulder. Younger did most, if not all, of the questioning and I answered everything. I was under the impression I was helping them piece together the jigsaw they'd been handed. I didn't know they'd already tagged me as the prime suspect.

They left the room and in came two more police officers who asked the same questions. And thus it went on in relay with a change of police officers every ten minutes or so. At one point I overheard an officer say he'd bet his wages that I would admit to it before the night was out. I was given one brief break, during which I ate a cheese sandwich and drank a cup of lukewarm tea, and then the circus started again. I was so tired that at one point, while Younger and Johnson were questioning me, one of them – I think it was Younger – shook me by the shoulder and said 'Don't go to sleep. We'll keep questioning you until you admit it.' I had even been refused access to a solicitor, to my family and to a phone call. Apparently, I was refused a solicitor because they said they were *only* questioning me.

After seven or eight hours of this merry-go-round, I was worn down and horribly tired. Then I found myself alone with PC Charlesworth, a man I'd known since childhood who had never liked me from day one. I believe they thought I'd break and spill it out to him. And they were right. There is only so much anyone can take and I'd had enough so I said I did it. I thought it would get them off my back and the next day they'd continue their investigations and ask why I'd lied to them. But it was not to be.

Charlesworth left the room, presumably to inform his superiors. Within a couple of minutes Younger and Johnson entered. It was Younger who broke the silence. 'I understand that you have told Mr Charlesworth that you have done it,' he said. I nodded and they started again asking the same questions. Even after the admission I wasn't informed of my rights or cautioned.

About an hour after I admitted it, Younger asked me how I got blood on my jeans. (Very observant these police officers. I had only been in the police station about eight hours!) I didn't realize I had until I looked down. I gave the only answer I could – that it had got on my clothing when I had knelt down by the side of Wendy Sewell (her identity had by now been established and made known to me). I also had blood on my hands which I knew about but when I'd asked PC Ball if I could wash it off, he'd said no. If I'd had anything to hide or fear I could quite easily have washed off the blood in any number of the water tanks dotted about the cemetery. I was also in easy distance of home and could have bathed and changed my clothing. Had I actually carried out the attack then surely I would have had blood on my person prior to leaving the cemetery to try and get a lemonade. And isn't it strange that I could pass Wilf Walker and his wife, Peter Moran and Charlie Carmen as well as stand only feet away from my mother, yet none said I had blood on my clothing either in their written statements or verbally to the police when questioned. Forensic examinations also stated that the blood on my jeans was not fresh but had got there after it had started to coagulate. However, I am digressing.

A uniformed officer stayed with me in the room for what seemed like half an hour and then in came Younger with my father. Finally, they'd informed my parents. My father was carrying a change of clothes for me and I was told the ones I was wearing would be required for a forensic examination. I don't know what he had been told, but he asked what was going on and I said I was being questioned about the assault on Wendy Sewell. They had told him that I had confessed, and I said that was right. He then said 'I am proud of you for owning up, but not for what you have done.' That comment has always stayed with me. We'd never been close as father and son; maybe that was partly due to his work, which took him away from home, first as an ambulance driver with irregular shifts and later as a long-distance coach driver. Somehow, his comment seemed to bridge that gap and make up for the time we'd lost together.

After ten minutes, they asked my father to leave and I sat there in my fresh clothes watched by the uniformed officer. After perhaps another half an hour, Younger came in with a man he introduced as a scenes of crime officer and said they would like to take my fingernail scrapings, which left my fingers sore, stinging and bleeding. After that I was asked to make a statement. My reading and writing were very poor and my spelling was atrocious, so when I was told I could write it or the officer would write it for me, I opted for the latter. It was a mistake I'll always rue.

As I dictated the statement, I was interrupted by Younger on several occasions who would make suggestions for inclusion. When I said that I had watched Wendy Sewell walking round the cemetery while finishing my cigarette, Younger said 'So you followed her?' 'No!', I said. 'I only watched her walk round.' 'No,' continued Younger, 'what I mean is you followed her with your eyes. It sounds better in the statement.' 'Yes, OK,' I replied. But it was written in the statement as *I followed her round the cemetery*. I could not have done this as it has been proved on numerous occasions by different people. There is no way I could have followed her round and, at the same time, left the cemetery to get some lemonade and be seen by Wilf Walker and his wife, Peter Moran, Charlie Carmen and my mother. But with the statement in the bag and my tired, scribbled signature sealing my fate I was led off to the cells.

I hadn't been there long when Charlesworth and another officer were sent to obtain hair samples for forensic examination. Then I was left alone for a couple of hours but, annoyingly, I was looked in on at regular intervals. I did voice my displeasure at one stage when a policewoman looked in but she said it was to prevent me from doing any harm to myself. I assured her that I had no intention of harming myself but to no avail, they kept looking.

The cell was disgusting. It measured about 10 foot (ft) by 7ft with a high vaulted ceiling, and it was illuminated by a dim bulb in a caged exterior security light. It smelt like a sty and the paint was chipped and flaking off. The bed, if indeed that is what it could be called, was a heavy wooden frame with planks attached, dirty and greasy from years of use. A dirty, thick, grey blanket was in one corner against the wall. Its smell made me queasy and I swear to God it was alive with all manner of infestations from overnight down and outs sleeping off their drunken stupors. I can only imagine where all its stains came from. In the other corner was a built-in toilet, which I guess was the height of luxury for its time, but a necessity to save the corners of the cell being used as a latrine. The end wall housed a heavy, steel window with thick glass bricks.

The next time they unlocked the door was to escort me to the reception deck and inform me that I was being taken to Buxton Police Headquarters. I caught a glimpse of the wall clock and saw that it was now 3.00 am. I had never seen so many police in one place before. I was handcuffed and led out to a waiting police van with blacked-out windows. On arrival, I was handed over to the duty staff who checked my identity and led me further into the station where I had my fingerprints and palm prints taken. Then followed the impossible task of trying to wash off the ink I was told would come off with soap and water. It didn't. I was led off to a holding cell and given a plastic mug of grey liquid that passed for tea. I took a cautious sip and the expression on my face said it all – it was viler than it looked.

Around half an hour later, the door opened and, with genuine apologies for the lack of comfort, an officer handed me a bundle of blankets to make a bed. Before he left he asked me for my belt and shoe laces but I had neither. He said it was to stop me hanging myself and then he bid me a hearty goodnight and closed the door. Goodnight! It had to be at least 5.00 am! I hoped that I wouldn't need to use the toilet as there wasn't one in the cell and I don't think I would have had a very nice reception had I rung the emergency bell on the wall. I counted the blankets and there were seven. With only a narrow concrete slab, no more than 18 inches wide and topped with wood, running the length of the outer wall I figured I would need to fold four blankets up to cushion against the hardness, fold one up for a pillow and the last two should double up to fend off the cold.

Despite the discomfort, I managed to sleep until 9.00 am when the door opened and I was offered breakfast. I am not normally one for breakfast but without knowing when I would be fed again and having eaten so little the day before, I accepted. I was given a plastic mug of the same grey liquid, lumpy porridge, two slices of bread drying at the edges and a sausage. I was then asked to surrender my boots. I protested as they had no laces in them but it fell on deaf ears. The floor was icy and the cell grew colder with each passing minute. There were no heating pipes or radiators in the cell, so if it was this bad in September God knows what it would be like in winter.

I was given a few paperback books to choose from to help alleviate the boredom. I have never much cared for sci-fi stories, but I found one that looked quite good and despite my poor reading ability I finished it in just over a day. I found myself another book but it didn't keep my interest and the rest of my time dragged. Lunch came about midday and was fish, chips and rock-hard peas with two slices of bread even dryer than at breakfast. By now, I had plucked up the courage to ring the bell and request the use of the toilet but I was told that I'd have to wait until staff came back from lunch. They obviously enjoy extended lunch breaks at Buxton HQ as I got the same answer an hour and a half later. I gave it about another hour before ringing the bell again and this time I was allowed out. The clock said 3.00 pm. I'd had to wait three hours. Dinner was served around 4.00 pm and was a fried egg with tinned tomatoes and two more slices of dry bread. I soaked it in the tomatoes to make it edible.

On Friday morning, I was taken to Bakewell Police Station where I was held for about an hour until I was put before Bakewell Magistrates' Court. I soon found out that this was to become a weekly occurrence until I was committed to the crown court. My first appearance before the magistrates was a short hearing with the police opening the procedures by announcing that they had no objection to my having bail. No sooner did they say that, my solicitor, Paul Anthony Gilbert Dickinson, told the magistrate he thought that his client might be better off on remand. So the beak, Harry Schofield, my former headmaster, remanded me for seven days in Risley Remand Centre.

Wendy Sewell's assault was reported in various local and regional newspapers. On Friday, 14 September 1973 under the headline *Murder Bid Charge*, one (probably the *Derbyshire Times*) wrote:

'Critically ill in Chesterfield Royal Hospital with serious head injuries is an attractive 32-year-old housewife, who was found unconscious in a Bakewell cemetery just after lunchtime on Wednesday. Yesterday morning, Derbyshire Police said that a young man had been charged with attempted murder and would appear at a special court in Bakewell later that day. The accused is understood to be 17-year-old Stephen Downing, a gardener from a Bakewell council estate. The woman, Mrs Wendy Sewell of Middleton-by-Youlgreave, was discovered just after 1.15pm. She was rushed to Chesterfield Royal Hospital but early yesterday morning had still not regained consciousness. Police are waiting at her bedside. She was discovered lying face downwards between grave stones in an old part of the churchyard, close to dense woodland. The cemetery was sealed off as police began their investigations.'

Wendy Sewell died that Friday without regaining consciousness and on Saturday, 15 September a post-mortem was carried out on her body. The following is an extract from the statement by the pathologist Alan Usher:

STATEMENT OF WITNESS
(C. J. Act, 1967, s.s. 2, 9; M.C. Rules, 1967, r. 7)

STATEMENT OF ___Alan USHER___

AGE OF WITNESS (if over 21 enter "over 21") ___Over 21.___

OCCUPATION OF WITNESS ___Home Office   Pathologist___

ADDRESS ___Consulting Rooms, Coroners Court,___

___Nursery Street, Sheffield.___

POST MORTEM EXAMINATION UPON:

Name: Wendey SEWELL   Sex: female   Age: 32 years   Office Worker

Address: Green Farm, Middleton by Youlgreave, Derbyshire.

Body identified by: Det. P.W. Price

Date and time of death: 2.35 p.m. Friday, 14th September, 1973.

Date and time of examination: 2.45 p.m. Saturday, 15th September, 1973.

Place of examination: The Mortuary, Royal Hospital, Chesterfield.

Observers present: Det. Chief Supt. Fryer; Det. Supt. Bayliss;
Det. Chief Insp. Johnson; D/C Oakes;
P.C. Ball and Mr. Biggin

. . . .

E X T E R N A L   E X A M I N A T I O N

The body was that of slimly-built white woman 5' 7" in height,

measuring 32.1/2" around the chest and weighing about 9.1/2 stones.

Hygiene:	very good; nails cut short and clean; no significant foreign material seen.
Hair:	appeared dark but head shaven as for surgery.
Eyes:	brown; right pupil dilated; left normal size. Left-sided subconjunctival haemorrhage most marked in the upper half of the eye; There was a little subconjunctival haemorrhage at the lateral angle of the right eye.
Mouth:	internal bruising of cheek on left side; own teeth in good condition.
Genitals:	'non virgo intacta' - the hymen vaginalis was markedly deficient in its posterior segment; no recent bruising or tears.
Anus:	One or two skin tags at the anal margin.
Rigor mortis:	intense and generalised.
Hypostatic lividity:	Poorly developed upon the back.

STATEMENT CONTINUATION FORM

STATEMENT OF .... Alan USHER ....

was left upon the path when the assailant made off.

Some time later, a witness saw SEWELL obviously badly hurt about the head lying amongst the graves some 25 feet away from the path. At this time she was seen to get to her feet and then fall across another grave striking her head. She was conveyed to a local hospital where it was realised that she had suffered such serious brain damage as to render the prognosis hopeless; surgery was accordingly confined to arresting haemorrhage and suturing the numerous wounds in the scalp. She died two days later without regaining consciousness.

My examination confirmed that she was previously in good health and I have found no natural disease which could have caused or contributed to her death.

She had been most violently assaulted almost certainly by someone using the pickaxe handle though some of her injuries might have resulted from kicking with heavy boots - in which case I would have expected her assailant to have blood upon his boots and/or trousers. At least seven or eight, and probably more, violent blows had been struck which smashed her skull, tore and bruised the underlying brain and caused massive bleeding into the brain coverings. The bruises about her arms indicate that initially she made some attempt to defend herself though the violence of the attack would rapidly overcome an unarmed person.

Indeed, the nature of the injuries to this woman's head and neck suggests that her assailant was in a frenzied state at the time of the incident. Though the removal of this woman's clothing below the waist seems to indicate a sexual motive for the attack, there is no real evidence to show that intercourse took place.

...ctions of lung showed some congestion and in places frank
...nage in the alvoli; the air passages were full of basophilic mucus.

MOUTH, THROAT AND NECK STRUCTURES

Mouth:	Own teeth in good condition; left cheek a little bruised.
Tongue:	normal; no brusing.
Larynx:	Hyoid bone and laryngeal cartilages intact; massive ecchymoses in the mucus membrane below the level of the false vocal cords.
Thyroid:	normal.
Carotids:	normal.
Cervical muscles:	some bruising of the deep cervical muscles.
Cervical spine:	intact.

The pathologist made clear that evidence suggested Wendy Sewell had been asphyxiated as there were bruises to her Adam's apple and back of neck as well as a bloody, frothy mixture in her lungs and airways. None of this evidence was presented by the police or prosecution to the judge or jury, or picked up by my defence at my trial or appeal in 1974. Had it done so this would have completely changed the direction of my trial. Instead it would take some forty years for this to surface.

After the hearing, I was taken back to the police station where I was able to see my solicitor. I said that the next time I was in court I would like to have bail but he insisted that I would be better off on remand. He was supposed to be acting in my best interest, so who was I to argue? For the next thirteen weeks I would make the trip to Bakewell every Friday for the hearing that was just a few minutes long. After the brief meeting with my solicitor I was permitted a one hour visit with my parents and sister in the holding cell that I had occupied originally at the police station. When my family left, I was cuffed and led out to a waiting police car, which took me to Risley Remand Centre.

Chapter 3

HMP 'Grisly' Risley
September 1973-May 1974

The first time I arrived at Risley in Warrington, Cheshire, I was escorted into reception by two police officers and asked my name by another. 'Stephen,' I said. 'What else?' he asked. 'Stephen Downing,' I said. 'Stephen Downing what?' he demanded. I told him my middle name, which made him stare at me with hatred in his eyes. One of the cops gave me a nudge and whispered 'Call him sir'. 'Don't prompt him, sir,' announced the hate-filled screw. 'Let the bastard learn the hard way.' Despite this, I answered all the remaining questions without calling anyone sir.

I was then sent through to the bath house, told to strip, handed a bathrobe, given a number (797501) and told to collect my clothes and have a bath. Asking for directions earned me a slap across the head and I was told to find my own way there. As I walked towards the baths, which were staffed by inmates, one of the reception screws yelled 'Nonce coming through.' Moments later a man was met by the bath house attendants who scooped him up and threw him in the end bath, which was scalding hot. After clambering out he staggered past

H.M. REMAND CENTRE

RISLEY

me naked and a hearty cheer went up. He was lobster red from head to toe. 'What was all that for?' I asked. I was told that he was a nonce – a rapist – and that was the treatment that awaited those offenders when they arrived. None slipped through the net as staff always announced the crime, loudly, so the inmates could hear. The word nonce comes from the acronym NONCE, which stands for 'Not of Normal Criminal Element' and was stamped on a sex offender's file.

When you arrive, your property and money are taken from you and placed in storage. If you want to buy some things, you give your order to the bath house inmate and choose from a selection on a wall chart. I ordered cigarettes, soap, toothpaste, orange juice and safety matches. I was advised to buy tobacco and rolling papers instead of cigarettes as it would last me longer, so I changed my order. I was told I'd receive my goods the next day.

Once I was bathed and dressed I was locked in a large holding cell at the far end of reception with other newcomers. There was no real seating, just concrete slabs that came out of the columns holding up the roof, and the walls were adorned with graffiti as well as discharges from every bodily orifice. I think we were there for about three hours. Some people had got into conversation, while others like me sat quietly looking at the walls and reading the scribbles from former inmates. When I, along with a number of others, had our names called, we were escorted through several locked gates to the prison hospital. There, we were handed over to another member of staff who apologized for the cramped conditions and said that it wasn't normally this bad. We were around forty on the ward when there should have been twenty-six but it was quite merry.

A week later the numbers reduced to normal and it became a lot less lively. However, the extra space meant large tables were returned to the centre of the ward so everyone sat playing cards, draughts and chess. A few gambled for tobacco and other worldly possessions. It was of course wholly against prison rules to gamble and also to exchange, give or sell on personal possessions, but most establishments allowed it to happen. A list of your possessions would be written on a property card. A property card is a record of all your personal belongings, including what is on your person and what is stored in reception, providing it will fit in your allocated storage box. If there's no room, it's sent off to Branston Stores. Branston is a massive storage depot that once belonged to Branston Pickle. The grounds are so vast, you get around them in a golf buggy. It is the main distribution centre for every conceivable item a prison needs to function: cups, cutlery, computers, clothing – you name it they have it. When property has been sent there, it can only be recalled once every twelve months by an inmate or by staff if you are being discharged. In the event of a transfer to another prison, all 'in possession' property is checked against the property cards and sent with you to your next establishment.

Property in transit after being checked is placed in plastic bags with a numbered security seal. The number is unique and traceable to the prison you have just left. In the early years, property was transported with you and reception kept everything that was not permitted, but in the mid to late 1980s the Home Office introduced sealed plastic bags and storage of property at Branston. In the 1990s they introduced 'volumetric control' which meant everyone was given two standard sized boxes and, with the exception of one large item, all personal possessions had to fit in these boxes. Anything over and above was handed to a visitor, mailed out or sent to Branston.

I was in the hospital ward because I was a potential suicide risk. Everyone on a murder charge was considered a suicide risk. I found a few 'friends' and we whiled away the days playing cards and telling jokes. My spell in hospital was the most comfortable time for me at Risley.

For thirteen weeks, until the committal papers were issued and the case was referred to Nottingham Crown Court, I visited the magistrates' court in Bakewell every Friday. I was then temporarily transferred to Lincoln Prison for the three-day hearing. Following committal, I was kept on remand and my family would visit me twice a week on Wednesdays and Fridays. Before this, they would visit on Wednesdays and then see me for a couple of hours at the police station after my return from the magistrates' court. Crown courts hear serious indictable offences such as robbery, rape and murder. A judge has overall responsibility for the court with a jury of twelve providing the verdict. My trial started at 9.00 am, 13 February 1973 at Nottingham Crown Court.

The prosecution outlined the case against me with one of their main planks being my 'doctored' and coerced voluntary statement. Judge Mr Justice Nield went on to explain: 'If the jury thought there had been oppression, any improper conduct by the police to induce this young man to make a statement, or to threaten him if he did not that such and such things would happen, then the statement is valueless.'

HMP Lincoln.

Nottingham Crown Court: the imposing view from the dock and public galleries.

INDICTMENT

The Crown Court at NOTTINGHAM

THE QUEEN - v - STEPHEN LESLIE DOWNING

STEPHEN LESLIE DOWNING

is charged as follows:-

STATEMENT OF OFFENCE

Murder

PARTICULARS OF OFFENCE

Stephen Leslie Downing on the 14th day of September 1973 in the County of Derby murdered Wendy Sewell.

Counsel
Prosecution - P. Bennett Q.C.
K. Matthewman
Defence - D. Barker Q.C.
J. Warren.

7. G. Parker
An Officer of the Crown Court

Date: 6th FEBRUARY 1974

13th February 1974

STEPEHN LESLIE DOWNING Arraigned

THE CLERK: Are you Stephen Leslie Downing?

STEPHEN LESLIE DOWNING: Yes.

THE CLERK: Stephen Leslie Downing you are charged in this indictment with murder. The particulars of the offence are that you on the 14th day of September 1973 in the County of Derby, murdered Wendy Sewell. Now, how say you to this charge, are you guilty or not guilty?

STEPHEN LESLIE DOWNING: Not guilty.

THE CLERK: Stephen Leslie Downing, the names you are about to hear called are the names of the jurors who are to try you. If, therefore, you wish to object to them or to any of them, you must do so as they come to the Book to be sworn and your objection shall be heard. Do you understand?

STEPHEN LESLIE DOWNING: Yes.

(Jury Sworn)

THE CLERK: Members of the Jury, the defendant, Stephen Leslie Downing is charged in this indictment with murder. The particulars of the offence are that he on the 14th day of September 1973, in the County of Derby, murdered Wendy Sewell and to this charge he has pleaded not guilty and it is for you to decide, having heard the evidence, whether he is guilty or not.

The judge outlined Wendy Sewell's and my movements during the material times as follows. Mrs Sewell left her employment at about 12.40 pm, making her way along Butts Road where she was seen by two witnesses. At about 12.45 pm another witness saw her from the main gate walking into the cemetery. Wilf Walker gave evidence and said that, at about 1.08 pm, he saw me strolling out of the gates with a pop bottle under my arm and he didn't notice anything about my clothing. Walker said that he saw me again at 1.15 pm, coming back to the main gate minus my pop bottle and, at 1.20 pm, I went to the lodge and reported that a woman had been attacked in the cemetery. Eric Fox and Fred Hawksworth also gave evidence and said that they had come into the cemetery in order to go to the store. The jury was then given an overview of what happened from there on by the witnesses involved. The rest of the day was taken up by the prosecution.

On 15 February 1974, Mr Justice Nield began his summing-up of the case which took up the remainder of the day and the jury was dismissed to consider the verdict. None of the following indicators to a miscarriage of justice trial were considered by my defence:

- Despite being only 17 years of age, I had been interviewed over many hours and denied a solicitor or the presence of an appropriate adult.
- My voluntary statement and 'confession' had been written down in pencil and then inked over after I had signed each page.
- The prosecution offered no evidence to show that whoever attacked Mrs Sewell had asphyxiated her before striking her with the pickaxe handle.

This farce of a trial lasted three days and concluded with my conviction.

Forensic scientist Norman Lee gave evidence and said that the blood found on me, the accused, could only have been present if I had been responsible for the assault. Lee described this evidence as a 'textbook example…which might be expected on the clothing of the assailant.' No full transcript of the trial exists, but it is known that, in summing-up, the judge drew attention to my admission during the trial of having indecently assaulted Sewell as she lay injured in the cemetery (I later denied that I had made those admissions during the trial).

The jury found me guilty of murder by unanimous verdict and I was sentenced to be detained indefinitely at Her Majesty's pleasure with a stipulation that I should serve a minimum of seventeen years. Caught in

FEMALE.

STEPHEN ELIE DOWNING

Date of Birth 4.3.56

Court NOTTINGHAM
Judge *field* J.
Justices

convicted / sentenced 15 Feb 74
Trial 13.2.74
14.2.74
15.2.74

Miss Hopwood + M.M

J. L. HARPHAM LTD
55 QUEENS STREET
SHEFFIELD

DEFENCE (LEGAL AID/PRIVATE)
Counsel P. Barker Qc.
J. Warren
Solicitors E. *mamo* + Co.
E. *Brushongate*, *Chesterfield*.

PROSECUTION
Counsel P. Bennett Qc.
K. Matthewman.
Solicitors
T. P. P. *London*.

Count	Offence	Plea	Verdict	Sentence or Order
	Murder	Not guilty	Guilty	To be detained during Her Majesty's Pleasure

an innocent prisoner's dilemma, I was unable to be paroled as I did not admit to the crime. I was classified as IDOM (In Denial of Murder) and therefore ineligible for parole under English law.

Following the sentencing, I was allowed two hours with my family and good friend Richard Brailsford. We were separated by a screen of wired glass, which had grills at either side for us to talk through. Everyone was shocked and stunned; it wasn't the outcome we had expected. I'm sure we talked about an appeal as I mentioned it to my solicitor, although he wasn't really interested. When our time was up, I was returned to Lincoln Prison where I stayed for a day or so before being transferred back to Risley. Instead of heading back to the hospital ward, I was told I would be going in one of the cells for my own protection as the inmates had seen TV news coverage of my case and were out to get me. I had never heard anything so ludicrous in my life but I had no say in the matter. The next day I met some of the people I had become acquainted with and when I put it to them they laughed, so together we went to the office to see if I could move back to the ward. The answer was still no. I would remain in the hospital cell for two weeks, with just the built-in radio for company, which piped cricket commentary in the day and Radio 1 at night, before being transferred to D Wing, which was home to the lifers.

When I arrived at D Wing I asked my family to bring me in a radio. Everyone would play the radio on Sunday evening to find out the chart position of their favourite band. The 1970s was a good time for music and I liked heavy rock bands such as Deep Purple, Black Sabbath and Alice Cooper. However, after two or three weeks I was offered tobacco for it. At first I kept refusing, knowing what the consequences would be if the staff found out, but in the end the offer of 3/4 ounce (oz) of tobacco was too good to turn down. It was agreed that I would hand over the radio after evening association at 8.00 pm. Association is when inmates integrate, watch TV and play games such as cards and snooker, pool and darts and it takes place every ten days for two hours. Within a few minutes of being locked up, I deeply regretted my decision, especially as I'd been handing out roll-ups like they were going out of fashion and my hoard had dwindled to the point that I was only left with enough to make half a dozen rollies for myself. I felt naïve and stupid and it hurt more when I heard that the recipient, who was being discharged the following day, had the radio confiscated at reception.

I decided to report the radio as stolen. The next morning, I went to work with the intention of announcing the crime at lunchtime. However, at about 10.00 am, a principal officer (PO), two or three senior officers (SO) and maybe a dozen uniformed staff walked in to the workshop and spoke to the civilian in charge of the workforce. I had a variety of menial jobs there, such as stripping the plastic sleeve from electrical wire and threading elastic on to papier-mâché masks. Wages were poor, just 30p a week, which was enough to buy 1/2 oz tobacco for 18p, a small box of safety matches for 3p and three packets of prison rolling papers (made by Rizla), which cost 1p per packet. Rizla brand papers were also available for 3p per packet. You could buy a few chews with the remaining 6p or you could carry it over to the next pay day.

My name was called out and the PO asked where my radio was. I lied and said it was in my cell. He swore at me and asked where it was and again I lied. The PO then put it to me that I had sold it and this had been confirmed by the man who bought it from me. What else could I do but admit it? The PO was far from pleased. 'You know what should happen to you, don't you?' he yelled. 'Yes!' I replied. 'What?' he asked and I said, 'Get a good kicking.' 'That's right,' he said before surprising me by adding, 'Well we can't get your radio back so consider yourself fortunate. Now get back to work and we'll hear nothing more about it.'

Wow! I was lucky. I had gone into a cold sweat as soon as they had walked in and an even colder one when they called out my name.

Discipline at Risley was meted out by the staff and usually consisted of between four and a dozen screws going into a cell and kicking the hell out of someone. Just about all the staff wore steel-toe capped boots and many had studs in the soles for good measure. There was also a cell within a cell on D Wing, made of concrete with thick glass bricks set in the ceiling of the inner cell, and above these was a 40-watt bulb. It was dim inside even with the doors open. A concrete slab with a grubby, straw-filled mattress and two heavy refractory blankets served as a bed, and a concrete post set into the floor was used as a stool. Aside from the blankets, the only moveable object was a heavily scaled, plastic chamber pot. Staff would put someone in this cell naked for three days, with only bread and water for breakfast, lunch and tea. Each meal consisted of three slices of bread with a pint of water. They were only allowed out of the cell to wash, shave and empty the pot in the morning and again in the evening. A bell push was set into the wall for summoning staff. It was a feature found in all cells but was not always answered. It is, by definition of the prison rules, there for emergency use.

D Wing housed those serving a life sentence or over ten years and like all the other wings was in a very poor state, mostly due to the inmates. I was lucky as I had an all-bar-one window, which was intact. Most had been broken and there was no point fixing them as they'd be broken again in no time at all. Few would use the chamber pots in their cells. Instead they'd urinate out of the window or make a parcel of faecal matter from newspapers or magazines and throw that out the window too. The smell was horrendous and a sea of sewage spread out from the outer wing walls and covered the floor for 6 to 8 feet. It was known as 'Shit Parcel Alley'. Anyone facing disciplinary action for whatever matter faced either a beating, being placed in the inner cell or both, and was made to clean up all the shit parcels from around the wings assisted by their cellmate (all cells, with the exception of D Wing, were occupied by two inmates). If you were lucky, you'd be issued with a spade while the other inmate carried the bin bag. I was only called on once to clean up and thankfully I was given a spade. Some were far less privileged.

There was also a women's wing adjacent to D Wing, which was separated by a wooden fence. By putting our heads out of the window, we could talk to each other and we'd get into conversations in the evenings, until the dog handlers patrolling the grounds told us to get our heads in and shut up. The only other contact I had with women was on Sunday mornings when we sat on the left-hand side of the chapel and they sat on the right. It is the only prison I know to preach to a full congregation. Staff would sit at the back and confiscate any notes that were seen being passed across the aisle.

It was difficult adjusting to the regime in D Wing as I was locked in my cell for eighteen hours a day. I'd been there about a week when I was visited by one of the SOs. He asked me how I was feeling and I said fine, but he wasn't convinced and said he was going to put me on evening association for a week to give me time to integrate with the other inmates. It was good to get out of such claustrophobic conditions and at the end of the week I tried to play on the depression so I could get out a bit more. I got away with it a couple of times but in the end, I realized I was just going to have to get used to it.

With the workshop pay so low, you did everything to eke out your tobacco, matches and papers. I'd split the matches lengthways with a pin or a razorblade squirrelled away from my morning shave; I was so desperate I even smoked the straw-like stuffing from my mattress. It was fatal to ask someone for rolling paper as it advertised the fact you had tobacco and invariably the cost of being given a paper would be to give them 'twos-up', that is to say give them half shares in it.

I had been on D Wing about two months when I was called into the SO's office and asked where I'd like to be transferred. I said I didn't know as it was my first time in prison. The SO said he had worked at a young offender's institution (YOI) called Swinfen Hall in Lichfield, Staffordshire and that it wasn't such a bad place. I thought anywhere must be better than Risley so I agreed. In one sense, I was going to miss Risley as I had learned its regime and had got to know a few people.

In April 1974, two months after my trial and conviction, a witness called Jayne Atkins said she saw me leaving the cemetery at the same time as she saw Wendy Sewell alive and unharmed and in the company of another man. She also said she saw a white van, which would have been Eric Fox driving into the cemetery. Not only does this confirm that Jayne Atkins was there that afternoon but it also corroborates my alibi that I was elsewhere at the time Wendy was attacked. I applied for leave to appeal on the grounds that I had a new witness.

Here are extracts from Jayne Atkins' witness statement made on 20 April 1974:

B

CRIMINAL APPEAL ACT, 1968

SEE NOTES ON BACK

(See R3 Form 6)

COURT OF APPEAL
CRIMINAL DIVISION **W**

NOTICE OF APPLICATION FOR
WITNESS ORDER
and/or
LEAVE TO CALL A WITNESS

To the Registrar, Criminal Appeal Office

REF. No. 128/B1/74

Royal Courts of Justice, Strand, LONDON, W.C.3A 2L

Write legibly in black

Particulars of APPELLANT	FULL NAMES Block letters	FORENAMES	SURNAME
	STEPHEN	LESLIE	DOWNING

ADDRESS
If detained give address where detained

H.M. REMAND CENTRE
WARRINGTON ROAD
RISLEY
WARRINGTON LANCS

INDEX NUMBER if detained

797501

Name and Address of witness:

MISS JAYNE ATKINS

Do you want a witness order?
(A witness order is not required if the witness would attend at the Court of Appeal voluntarily).

Please see letter

Was the witness called at the trial?

NO

The witness can now give the following evidence (which he did NOT give at the trial):—

TO THE EFFECT THAT SHE WAS IN THE CEMETARY AT THE RELEVANT TIME, SAW THE DECEASED, THE ACCUSED + A THIRD PERSON WHOSE IDENTITY IS NOT KNOWN. SHE SAW THE ACCUSED LEAVE THE CEMETARY, THE DECEASED + THE THIRD PARTY REMAINING THEREIN

The evidence was not given at the trial for the following reasons:—

THIS WITNESS HAD NOT THEN BEEN TRACED HER EVIDENCE HAS ONLY JUST COME TO LIGHT

S Downing
(Signed)   (Appellant)

DATE
16/4/74

Address of person signing on behalf of Appellant (See Note 5)

CRIMINAL APPEAL
FOR USE IN THE CRIMINAL APPEAL OFFICE
Received
RECE...

W

Form 1460 31571—18-9-70

On 25 October 1974, the Court of Appeal reached the conclusion that Jayne Atkins' evidence of seeing Wendy Sewell walking towards the back of the consecrated chapel was unreliable due to some trees obstructing her line of sight. The court, and in particular Lord Justice Orr, felt that it was not credible and secure enough, as she had not mentioned this information until after my conviction. Some twenty years later, Jayne said the reason that she had not come forward sooner was because at the time she was a vulnerable 15-year-old girl and said, 'I was afraid the man in the cemetery might have recognized me and I might be the next one!'

I knew Stephen Leslie DOWNING, he lived quite close and I saw him often just to say "hello" to. I knew that he sometimes worked in the Cemetery, looking after the graves.

I remember the day that Wendy SEWELL was attacked in Bakewell Cemetery. I was at school that day, and I went home for my lunch as usual. My mother was knocking about somewhere, had probably gone to the shop before it had shut. My brother and sister were out playing. At about five to one, one of the children came in and let our cross-bred mongrel dog out. I listened to the one o'clock news, fetched the dog's lead and went to look for the dog. That would be about 1.5 p.m.

I went down the road towards the Cemetery and looked over the wall into the Garden of Remembrance. I didn't see the dog, but I saw a girl walking at the back of the Garden of Remembrance at the point I have marked "A" on the map showing Bakewell Cemetery. I produce the map to which I have attached a label marked JEA 1 which I have signed. She was walking in the direction of the arrow.

The girl was about 5' 8" with dark shoulder length hair. She was wearing a fawn coloured trouser suit and a dark pullover. The trousers were slightly flaired. She was alone. I did not see anyone else at that time.

(Signed) J. Atkins.

STATEMENT CONTINUATION FORM

Form 50

STATEMENT OF___Jane Elizabeth ATKINS____

I walked towards the gap in the wall and looked round for the dog, but couldn't see it. I went through the gap and along the footpath which runs parallel to Burton Edge, and then turned right onto the footpath in front of the Unconsecrated Chapel. I stopped in front of the Unconsecrated Chapel and then saw the same girl in the fawn trousers suit, standing on the footpath between the rear of the Consecrated Chapel and the Woodshed, at the point on the map, produced marked JEA 1 where I have put a cross marked "B". She was facing towards the Woodshed. There was a man standing immediately in front of her, facing her, and he had both hands round her waist, talking to her. The girl did not seem to be agitated and I got the impression they were just talking. The man was about the same height or a little taller than the girl, with collar length sandy coloured hair. He was wearing a blue boiler suit with a blue denim jacket. I didn't see his face.

I was still looking for my dog. I then saw Stephen Leslie DOWNING. He was walking towards the main gate along the centre footpath at the point on the map JEA 1, where I have marked "C". I recognised him by his walk. He was dressed in blue denim jeans and jacket. He was walking with his arms by his side and, so far as I could see, he was not carrying anything. I did not look again to see if the girl and man were still together. Between the time I saw the girl and the man together, and when I saw Stephen Leslie DOWNING, I was looking round for my dog, and it would be no more than a couple of minutes between seeing the girl and man together and then seeing Stephen.

I was standing at the point marked D on the map JEA 1. I then went back to the Garden of Remembrance where I found my dog. She ran off towards the bottom corner of Catcliff Wood. I caught

38

STATEMENT CONTINUATION FORM

Page No. 3

STATEMENT OF Jane Elizabeth ATKINS

14

her, and went along the footpath at the edge of the Cemetery towards Burton Edge.

As I was going from the Cemetery onto the footpath at the corner by Catcliff Wood, I heard a vehicle and I saw a white van, which I took for the Council van, come along the Central Drive in the Cemetery towards the Unconsecrated Chapel. I heard a man's voice shout, but I don't know what he was shouting.

I carried on along Burton Edge to home. I put the dog in the house. No-one was at home. I then walked back to school, but saw no-one I knew.

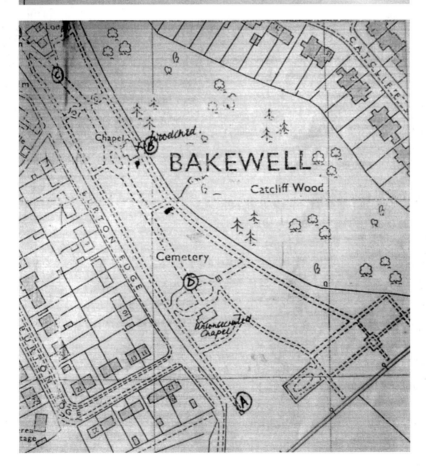

Chapter 4

HMP Swinfen Hall
May 1974-January 1978

I was in for a shock when I arrived at Swinfen Hall as the staff were relaxed towards inmates and didn't resort to bullyboy tactics. It was a Borstal when it first opened in 1963 but became a long-term young offenders' institution in 1972. It housed 182 young prisoners serving medium and long-term sentences and consisted of 174 cells and eight dormitories, and was well staffed with around one officer for just over two inmates.

After being checked in and escorted to my wing, I was asked a few basic questions about my diet and religion and informed of a few basic

HMP Swinfen Hall near Lichfield, Staffordshire.

The dining room at Swinfen Hall.

rules. For the rest, as is always the case, I'd have to ask staff or learn from the inmates. I was taken up to my cell on the mezzanine floor. As a lifer I wasn't allowed to be housed on the floor below or above, to make it more difficult to tunnel out. The outside back wall was also reinforced.

One of the better things about Swinfen Hall was that evening association took place every night from 6.00 to 9.00 pm. On weekends, association was from 10.00 am until 1.00 pm, then we were locked up for an hour while staff had their lunch. We were unlocked from 2.00 to 5.00 pm, locked up while staff dined and we were out again from 6.00 to 9.00 pm. During association the wing gates were left open so you could visit friends on other wings. It was also the opportunity to call in the library, read the papers, attend educational classes or visit the chapel. Risley didn't have a library, just a cupboard with a few books in it, and most of them had pages missing. On Saturday mornings, the chapel would screen a film for the young prisoners (YPs) who were under 18 and it would be screened again for the adults in the afternoon. All the films were chosen by the vicar, so nothing gratuitous was shown.

Time seemed to fly by as there was so much to do. Although I hadn't been academic at school, I enrolled in a number of classes, including

Art, Spoken German, Woodwork, Technical Drawing and Drama. I also had two sessions of English in the day. I did all I could to improve my poor reading skills and educate myself. I would pore over the letters I received from my solicitors and copy their style in my letters back to them. I would also write to my family as often as I could. We were granted one free letter a week with postage paid from public funds (another privileged letter, issued for good behaviour, could also be given). I tried to get on the Painting and Decorating course on several occasions, but each time I was informed that, as a lifer, I would have plenty of opportunity in the future to do the course so the place should go to a short termer. They trained twelve inmates every three months but I was never successful so in the end, I stopped applying.

I also worked in a workshop that produced audio tapes. At first I was on the assembly line that put the cassettes together, which was hard work as we produced 1,000 a day. This paid the princely sum of £1.98 per week but it was better than the job I was given on arrival, which was wing cleaner and paid 60p a week (still double what I got at Risley). I was like a kid in a sweet shop. The canteen (prison shop) had a much bigger selection than Risley and I bought everything I needed and still had money left over. Of course, it wasn't long before I was buying more tobacco and smoking heavily.

Unfortunately, the cassette tape work was stopped by security as they believed it was possible for inmates to record on to them, although quite how we would achieve this is beyond me as we were only permitted standard medium wave and long wave radios. Instead we were given small plastic cowboys, Indians and soldiers to hand paint. There was no set amount; we just had to produce as many as we could and in return we were given £1.98 per week. That job came to an end after we had painted about 250,000 and then we started putting tyres on to plastic pram wheels. That was a short-lived job and then we removed surplus rubber from car seat covers, which were fresh from their moulds.

After two years in the same workshop, I was in need of a change and so I was transferred to the workshop downstairs. The work there was much better and there was more money to be earned. We assembled the webbing for car seats under contract to Pirelli but that came to an end and it was turned into a contract services workshop, which meant that if a firm offered a contract that was considered suitable and conformed to the security level required, it would be accepted. There was also a two-week break between jobs and although we were still expected to go into work, we just played cards and drank tea. If the weather was good we would go on to the sports field to play cricket. Norman, the officer instructor from my first workshop, was an ex-professional cricketer, and the instructor from contract services shop was an ex-professional rugby player called John.

I found it a good deal easier to make friends at Swinfen Hall. Titch, so called due to his diminutive stature, was just 15 years old. He was serving a life sentence for stabbing a bloke with a combat knife three weeks after leaving school. We used to talk about getting ourselves a Harley-Davidson each and touring Europe and America. At the time, I think we both believed that it would happen, although my dreams faded when Titch failed to write after I moved to another prison. We were both friends with a lifer called Ginger who had red hair. We pooled our wages, which meant we were able to enjoy a few luxury items that you couldn't afford on your own unless you were a non-smoker or you were lending out tobacco to barons for a 'double back'. It was easy to get into serious debt with the barons. It worked like this: if you borrowed 1/2 oz of tobacco, you paid 1 oz back the following week. Failure to pay it back meant it was doubled and became a debt of 2 oz. Some people sold off personal possessions – irreplaceable items bought for them by their family – to pay the barons. I came across quite a few inmates who had been disowned by their families for doing that.

There was an ever-growing number of debtors who, for their own protection, wanted to go on 'Rule 43', which meant they would be segregated from other prisoners. At one point the PO on C Wing, which housed most of the debtors, insisted they told him who they owed tobacco to and how much. Then he took the baron into his office and said he would receive the amount owed, at a rate of 1 oz a week, until it was paid off. Neither he nor any of his friends were to lay a finger on the debtor. Normally the debtor would have been placed on Rule 43 and then transferred to another prison and the baron would be placed on governor's report and adjudicated the following day.

Unlike Risley, Swinfen Hall put all of its adjudications before a governor. Adjudication is very much like a small court hearing, and some might say there is no difference between adjudication and a court hearing as the governor and his staff are always right and the inmate is always guilty. Punishments (or 'awards' as the governor and Home Office prefer to call them) vary from a caution through to several days in the segregation unit and often a loss of one, several or all privileges. The only items that cannot be removed are library books, newspapers and access to letter-writing materials. The sole exception to this is when a person is placed on the F2052SH – a self-harm register – and medical staff, in consultation with the governor, decide that it is in the inmate's best interest for certain items to be restricted.

I had been pals with Titch and Ginger for about six months when Ginger was released. Titch and I pooled our wages and lived just as comfortably as when we were three. I was in the cell next to Titch and after lock-up, I was able to chat with him out of the window or through the small gap under the heating pipes. During association, we would watch some TV or sit in the cell chatting about music, work, education, life in general and our future plans on our Harley-Davidsons, which passed many a long hour.

I was 19 years old and quite clearly suffering from post-traumatic stress disorder (PTSD), of which little was known. A prison report prepared around this time described me as the following:

> 'A dull, lifeless and emotionally immature young man, who never displayed any feelings but could be stubborn at times. On arrival he had been at a loss, moving around like someone in a dream. He would not speak unless approached and even then would only answer in monosyllables. He had eventually found a comfortable niche and since then had been content to remain in the background, not making any real attempt to improve himself, or to make use of the facilities offered. His work record was poor and he continued to give the impression he was on another level and was oblivious to what was going on around him. He was polite and friendly enough in his dealings with staff, though with little to offer by way of conversation. His continued denial of guilt for the offence precluded him from gaining true insight. Overall, he made little progress, though he was able to cope generally.'

I was also experiencing physical pain due to a fall I'd had at school. The base of my spine was agonizing and there was discharge there. I had complained of this while on remand but the doctor simply recommended I did extra gym activities, although I was granted a shower and change of underwear every day instead of once a week. I had put off seeing another doctor for as long as I could, worried I'd be met with the same diagnosis. But I was wrong. The doctor informed me that it was pilonidal sinus (a growing abscess under the skin) and asked if I would like to have an operation. I said that I would and arrangements were made for me to be transferred to HMP Walton in Liverpool. Two weeks later, in September 1976, I was taken to Walton's hospital. I recall meeting with the surgeon and the anaesthetist, receiving the pre-med injection, being wheeled off to theatre, the anaesthetic being administered and waking up that evening to be given a cheese omelette and a glass of milk. It wasn't until the next day that the other patients told me I'd nearly pegged it. Apparently, I'd been vomiting uncontrollably and a mad panic had set in as they scrambled to find a ventilator (the first two having failed to work). I wasn't at all worried by this, after all I was still alive, but out of curiosity, and not sure if the other patients were just having a joke, I asked the ward sister if it was true and she said yes. I'd fallen madly in love with this woman and discovered she was 30 and divorced. I proposed to her from my bedside and was devastated when she turned me down.

When I returned to Swinfen Hall following my treatment, I really noticed the noise emanating from the windows. I was as bad as everyone else, as I enjoyed a chat out of the window, especially on a hot summer's night. Most would call it a night at 10.00 pm as the cell lights were put out. Some night patrols would shout 'Lights out in five minutes', which gave you time to make your bed and roll a few cigarettes. It was policy here to make a 'bed pack' each morning before going to work, which was considered good disciplinary practice and allowed the bed to be aired. The two sheets and three blankets were folded into a square and placed at the head of the bed. Cell inspections would take place on Saturday mornings and anyone not up to scratch had to do it again and ring their cell bell to have it inspected again. If you were doing educational studies, you could submit an application for an extension until 11.00 pm. However, some inmates would be shouting to each other until the early hours.

I would be four years into my sentence, and 21 years old, before I would be considered eligible for review for parole. At the time I didn't know my tariff had been set at seventeen years, as it was Home Office policy not to disclose what the Lord Chief Justice had set as the tariff for detention and retribution. In hindsight, there was no way I'd get parole on the first attempt. In fact I would not be eligible for parole until I had served the tariff period. It was therefore little more than a paper exercise for the staff, just like the F75 report, which was a review carried out every twelve months on lifers. Although this was meant to be the first step to parole, it was a routine matter, as most of us were unlikely to qualify for that.

Until an inmate is 21, they are classed as being a young prisoner and reside in a YP's institution. After this they are 'starred up' to an adult facility, be that an adult wing of a mixed prison or an adult prison. I was starred up at 21, but didn't transfer until I was 22.

Chapter 5

HMP Wakefield: 'Monster Mansion' January 1978-August 1980

Category A prisoners and escapees are only given a few minutes' notice before being transferred and are not told of their destination so they can't inform anyone who may help them abscond. Anyone of a lower category is considered less likely to make an escape and is therefore informed beforehand. I started off as a Category B prisoner so I had time to let my family know that I was moving to HMP Wakefield, which is located in Wakefield itself. Known for its large number of lifers, it is the biggest high-security prison in Western Europe and is known as Britain's toughest jail.

Inside Wakefield Prison.

My single cell was on the top landing (lifers weren't permitted to share) and after depositing my belongings I went exploring. I hadn't been on the wing long when I was approached by a couple of inmates who I'll call Harry and John. Harry was the most talkative and he took me round the wing, introducing me to various people. We stopped off at one cell and were invited in after knocking on the door. I was told that was the polite thing to do in adult prisons. I was given a cup of tea and made very welcome by the cell's occupant, Andy. I became good mates with Harry and John who pooled their wages so that they would go further, and within a week I was invited to pool mine with theirs. I accepted and each Monday evening we would sit in a cell and work out what we would need for the coming week.

I was located on A Wing, which got 'canteened' (when the items you had bought were delivered) on Tuesday nights. On Mondays, everybody went to the canteen and got paid. All you could buy was 1/2 oz of tobacco, a packet of rolling papers, a box of matches or a packet of flints for use in a (bought or homemade) tinder lighter. I had a tinder lighter at Swinfen Hall, but now I was able to buy a metal one made by some of the inmates in the welding shop. Most would sell them for 1/2 oz of tobacco. You could buy wicks at the canteen but they didn't work very well, so almost everyone plaited some strands from a mop head. Smoking with such rudimentary equipment could be dangerous. That year, there was a major fire at Wakefield, which led to fire-retardant mattresses being introduced in all prisons.

You stuck with your friends and tried to find your own place. D Wing was known as the married quarters as the bulk of the inmates there were practising homosexuals. Most of the people I associated with, including Harry and John, were located on the second landing. I learned that to get a cell on that landing, the most coveted of all, I would need to make a wing application. I was quite a long way down the waiting list but after about three or four weeks, I was told to pack my kit and move down. Harry, John and I were able to keep a watch on each other's cell as stealing was rife. While up on the top landing I had all my records stolen, and despite reporting it, I was told I 'should learn to take more care' of my property. The wing had a communal record player, which could be booked for two one-hour sessions during unlock in the evening or weekend.

At first I worked as a wing cleaner but after three or four weeks, I acquired a job in the heavy fabrics shop making water bottle covers and rifle slings for armies around the world. We also made white felt aprons for the General Post Office, which used them in the sorting rooms and occasionally, we were lumped with the mundane job of making mail sacks from grey polyester. The money was quite good and certainly higher than I had received at Swinfen Hall. Top pay was about £3.75 and it wasn't long before I was earning that.

When we received a contract to make tarpaulin truck covers and haystack covers I was offered the job of machinist. The truck covers were 30ft by 21ft and the stack covers were 50ft by 50ft, and the huge machine we were sent had a three-speed gearbox, a hand-operated clutch and instructions written in old German. Two inmates managed to translate some of it as they spoke the language, although not old German. In the end someone from the company had to come out and show us how to get it operational. The contract was for fifty of each cover and while we started off making one a day, we got it off to such a fine art, we could do two a day in the end.

At the end of the contract, I got a job that involved sweeping, emptying bins, cleaning and moving things from one place to another. The money was a massive drop to £1.98 so it was hard to get by each week, but I got used to it. I didn't mind cleaning windows, but I refused to hang from the bars 30ft up to clean those in the governor's office. I was alone in demanding a ladder and safety harness as the rest of the team had no objection at all to risking their lives. I think they neglected to realize the prison would not have given a hoot if any of them had fallen, and nor would the Home Office have paid out any compensation.

My family would visit every two weeks for two hours. Occasionally, if my father was away on a driving job, it would be three weeks between visits. Wakefield had the best visiting room of all the prisons I have graced, as spanning the width of the lower end of the room were floor to ceiling aviaries with a variety of finches, budgies and cockatiels. There were also large tanks filled with tropical fish. One was even full of piranhas. It was fascinating to watch them make short work of fresh meat with their needle-sharp teeth and frenzied gluttony. Wakefield was renowned for breeding tropical fish and exporting them all over the world, and I developed a keen interest in the subject.

Quite a lot of the men would keep budgies or occasionally a cockatiel in their cells. They had to be bought from one of the staff, who bred the birds, and I placed an order for a budgie. A new lot had just hatched and I was told that they would be ready in about four weeks. When I got called to the SO's office, I was handed a box and told to take one and return the other two. I got back to my cell and looked into the box cautiously. They were tiny and as I tried to carefully scoop up the one I liked the best, it wriggled away and I ended up with what looked like the smallest and weakest of the trio. Not wanting the other two to get out the box, I kept the runt and returned the box to the office. I'd already acquired a wooden cage that had been made in prison and so back in my cell, I began to make a fuss of my new companion. I needed a name for the little chap and on close inspection, I noticed his feet were much smaller than an average budgie of his size so I called him Flatfoot. It would be another week before he could fly so I was able to become good friends with him and he learned that I could be trusted. I got into the habit of putting him in his cage at 10.00 pm, where he would have some seed and then settle down for the night. One evening I was so engrossed in a book, I hadn't noticed the time and saw he'd put himself in his cage of his own accord. From then on, I noticed he went to bed like clockwork at 10.00 pm – he had his ritual and I had mine. I left the cage door open for him to come and go as he pleased; it was the nearest I could give him in terms of freedom. I knew I needed a metal cage as otherwise I wouldn't be able to take him with me when I left. I wrote to my family and asked if they would send me some money and a few days later I received a letter with £25. I then made an application to have a cage bought for me as a member of staff would go out each week and make 'outside' purchases for inmates.

On one occasion Flatfoot was unwell. Fortunately, one inmate's visitor was a vet and if a bird fell ill he was happy to stop by and cast his professional eye over it. He diagnosed gastroenteritis and suggested that I put him on a course of penicillin seed, so I ordered some the next morning. Getting a bird to eat medicated seed is not easy but I nursed him back and thankfully he made a full recovery.

As time went on, Harry got parole and was discharged and I stopped having much to do with John, who had become rather moody. I had got to know some of the staff quite well and was on first name terms with them. Many of them treated me as a human being rather than just a surname, number or statistic. Most of the names elude me now although I recall the workshop instructor, Bob Benge, and a young man called Paul Beaumont (both uniformed prison officers). Unfortunately, not all were nice. One of the most hated screws was SO Ducker, a thoroughbred bastard if ever there was one. I and many others, including members of staff, enjoyed the day he got balled out by the chief officer. It all started after the chief asked for volunteers to clean up some human waste after a soil pipe had burst. Several came forward and were kitted out with overalls, gloves, masks and boots together with whatever tools were needed for the job and the instructions that everything was to be incinerated afterwards. With the work complete, the chief ordered a screw to take the volunteers to the canteen where each was to be given a bar of soap, bottle of shampoo and 1 oz of tobacco, before taking an early shower and having the rest of the day off. However, when they got there, Ducker ordered them out and said that they'd get nothing. When the chief heard this he came out of his office, bellowed Ducker's name and told him to get his arse into the centre, now! They then stood nose to nose as the chief screamed at him for several minutes.

The chiefs were the fine line between 'us and them' (the inmates and the staff). The chief was the inmate's ally and the governor's right-hand man. When there were adjudications, it was the chiefs who informed the governor of any previous peccadillos and when it came to punishment, the governor would always ask the chief his opinion and accept the chief's suggestion. It was a sad day when they did away with the chief ranks and introduced more governor grades.

Wakefield was known as Monster Mansion because it housed so many dangerous criminals, and while I did make friends, you had to watch your back. One notable prisoner who was on my wing the same time as me, and whom I spoke to on numerous occasions, was Robert Maudsley, who was responsible for the murders of four people, three of which were committed in prison. He was nicknamed Hannibal the Cannibal after allegedly eating part of the brain of one of the men he killed in prison, although this was later disputed. Before Wakefield, he was sent to Broadmoor Hospital for the criminally insane, which is where, in 1977, he and another inmate took a prisoner hostage and tortured him to death.

One afternoon in 1978, while a friend and I were in the community room listening to music after a morning working in the heavy fabrics shop, Maudsley murdered two inmates. The first he lured into his cell, garrotting and stabbing him before hiding the body under his bed. He then went on the prowl for his second victim whose skull he hacked at with a makeshift dagger before smashing his head against the wall. After doing so, he put his belongings into a pillow case, went calmly to the SO's office, placed the dagger on the desk, told them that the next roll call would be two short and asked to be taken to the 'block' (segregation wing). Staff didn't believe him and told him to stop being stupid and go and get his lunch. The reality sank in when it came to locking everyone up and they were indeed two short. All hell broke loose. It was obvious that he'd had assistance, if only in making the knife in one of the metal workshops. The attacks were rumoured to be so vicious that one was left with his head hanging by a thread and the other was impaled on the bed so fiercely that it took two men to remove him. I don't know how much truth there is in the second part as he could have only been pinned to the mattress.

In 1983, Maudsley was deemed too dangerous for a normal cell so a two-cell unit was built in the basement of Wakefield Prison. To this day, he's confined in a 'glass cage', similar to the one featured in the Hannibal Lecter film *Manhunter*. A solid steel door opens into a cage within the cell, which is encased in thick Perspex. It's furnished with a table and chair made out of compressed cardboard, a toilet and sink, which are bolted to the floor and a concrete slab for a bed. He remains there twenty-three hours a day. During his daily hour of exercise, he is escorted to the yard by six prison officers and is not allowed contact with any other inmates.

On another occasion, a member of staff was found to have smuggled a handgun and ammunition inside. This was something of an embarrassment to the Home Office and not something that it would, I'm sure, like to see in print again. Unsurprisingly, after Maudsley ran riot, people started fitting security chains to the insides of their doors. This was frowned upon by staff as they wouldn't be able to gain entry in an emergency. They did, however, allow us to attach heavy leather straps, which we would pinch from the workshop.

Like many old prisons, Wakefield, the original part of which was built in 1594, has a gruesome past. In the seventeenth and eighteenth centuries, many offenders, men, women and children, would be beheaded and their heads impaled on stakes outside the gates as a deterrent to would-be criminals. The current buildings date back to Victorian times and the general fabric has changed little since then.

On 27 January 1979, *The Spectator* ran a piece called 'Crisis in the Prisons', which described the environment at the time:

'During one recent summer, there were approximately fifteen hundred inmates in Liverpool prison, a Victorian building which had been designed originally for one thousand men. There were only twenty officers on duty on a long, hot night; and then the banging started. The prisoners thumped on the walls, the doors, the bars. The whole prison reverberated to this concerted demonstration against the sheer numbers, the heat, the smell, the proximity. The landing shook under the officers' feet, and the noise didn't stop.

'Roy Jenkins, when he was Home Secretary in 1975, declared that a prison population of 42,000 would place the whole system in a state of crisis – that, in other words, it would cease to work... . Last year the Prison population had reached 42,155 and there are no signs of it diminishing. For every prisoner in custody before the war, there are now three. No new prisons were built in this country between 1918 and 1958. Of the fifty six closed prisons, only thirteen have been built since 1914. It is as if we were still trying to fight our domestic battles on horseback... . For the majority of prisoners in this country, conditions are actually worse than those which the Victorians intended to create; and this situation is deteriorating all the time.

'The men now "going inside" tend to be younger and more violent; they are also more sophisticated, questioning the whole nature of authority and punishment. In Wakefield prison, a "dispersal prison" designed for lifers and highly dangerous 'Category A' prisoners, there are 150 inmates under the age of 25. Such men tend to be angry and watchful; they have very little left to lose. It should be remembered that even a highly secure prison like Wakefield can only be administered on the sufferance of the prisoners themselves.

'Under these conditions, prison officers themselves will naturally tend to become more anxious and aggressive. But it may be significant that I have heard very few criticisms from prisoners about the older officers in the prison service; most complaints concern the behaviour of the younger staff.

These young officers are part of the silent revolution in the prison system, as it becomes both more technocratic and more impersonal.'

Some would argue that this environment is good enough for the kind of people who go out and commit offences. But surely, the offender's punishment is being sent to prison to have their freedom forfeited, they are not sent there to be punished by the officers. One establishment that believed in hard tactics, and appeared to be a law unto itself, is HMP Dartmoor, but more of that later.

One evening in August 1980, I returned from work to be told I should pack my belongings as I was being transferred the next day to HMP Gartree in Market Harborough, Leicestershire. It came as a shock as I expected a little more notice and I wasn't able to inform my family who were due to visit that weekend. I rushed around the wing looking for boxes so I could pack. At the same time, I tried to find out what Gartree was like. As usual I heard good and bad stories, so I knew I was going to have to wait and find out for myself. I figured that having survived 'Grisly Risley' I could live anywhere. As I packed up my belongings, I knew space would be tight. I desperately wanted to take all my wood veneers with me, but I just didn't have the means to carry them, so they had to stay. It was a shame as some were exotic and very expensive.

Chapter 6

HMP Gartree
August 1980-September 1985

As I passed through Gartree's reception, I was handed the customary second-class letter at public expense and a visiting order application. I filled it in and told the wing SO I was expecting a visit from my family at the weekend and hadn't time to inform them of my move. The SO asked for their phone number, dialled it and passed the phone to me. I told them of my move and the officer gave them directions to Gartree. At least they wouldn't have a wasted journey.

In the 1980s HMP Gartree was considered to be one of Britain's toughest prisons. A high-security dispersal prison, it housed some of the nation's worst offenders including paedophiles and child killers. Moors murderer Ian Brady, who was convicted with Myra Hindley of killing five children in 1966, was transferred to the hospital wing just before I left. A former prison officer, Tim Cousins, recalled hearing a commotion coming from Brady's cell one night. When he peered through the spyhole, he said Brady was 'creeping around his cell saying "They're only kids, I don't know what the fuss is about."'

Gartree was considerably more modern than Wakefield and the accommodation was somewhat more habitable, although the cells were smaller. At least the windows were at waist height and offered views, even if some were of brick walls. The windows at Wakefield were about 6 ft from the floor, with two very small panes of glass, which were so grimy you couldn't see through them. The windows at Gartree were large and had a centrepiece that opened, although there were bars across to prevent anyone getting through.

The padded chairs in the TV room were a luxury I had not experienced before. Association was every evening and each wing had its own video recorder with someone responsible for recording decent films and TV programmes, which would then be shown in the evenings and throughout the day at weekends. This was a first for me.

Gartree was quite small and it was also well staffed. In April 1982, it was recorded as having 174 prisoners and 202 prison officers although the number of prisoners increased to 219 just over a year later due to building works. When I arrived, there were four wings located on two upper floors and fifty-nine cells on each level. The lower floor was devoted to offices, association rooms, the servery (for meals) and the bath house. There was also a cooker for anyone wanting to prepare a meal. Wakefield also had Baby Belling cookers on the wings, but they were in high demand, especially at the weekend when a number of people would make a curry supper. I got on particularly well with some Asian inmates who always gave me a spice mix for our Saturday night feast. The cooker at Gartree was seldom in use as no one clubbed together to make a meal and the food served up at mealtimes was plentiful, filling, tasty and wholesome. It was the same at Wakefield where you could help yourself to unlimited fresh salads and vegetables. You couldn't say the same about Risley and Dartmoor where the food wasn't fit to be served as pigswill.

Around eighteen months before I arrived, there had been a riot and the inmates had taken control of the prison, assaulting and injuring some staff and smashing the place up. Eventually the inmates surrendered but the damage was so bad, 150 of the 298 prisoners had to be moved to other jails. When I arrived at Gartree I was sent to one of the only two wings that had survived the riot. About a month later, it was announced that everyone on the wing was to pack all their belongings as we would be transferring to one of the newly refurbished wings. At first we protested but the move wasn't too bad and at lunch we shared a cold buffet with the staff. This was welcomed because the only time you got to 'share' anything with staff was during a football match when inmates played against them, but even then only eleven players plus a reserve or two would play. I was never a spectator – I can't stand watching the game!

At Gartree, I shared a wing with the only surviving terrorist from the Iranian Embassy siege. The siege made worldwide news when it took place between 30 April and 5 May 1980, after six armed men stormed London's Iranian embassy and took twenty-six people hostage. They demanded the release of Arab prisoners from jails in Khuzestan and their own safe passage out of the UK but the British government turned them down.

When a hostage was murdered, the Special Air Service (SAS) entered the building by abseiling from the roof and killed five of the six terrorists. The remaining terrorist, Fowzi Nejad, was now down the corridor from me and would serve twenty-seven years in various prisons. He was pointed out to me and, like others, I made an effort to speak to him but either he didn't understand English or he chose to ignore us all. Before long he was transferred elsewhere.

I would, however, meet the men accused of the Carl Bridgewater murder, known collectively as 'the Bridgewater Four'. The four – Patrick Molloy, James Robinson and cousins Michael and Vincent Hickey were all likeable but I got to know James the best. We would chat or just watch TV together. The Bridgewater Four were tried and convicted of killing 13-year-old paperboy Carl Bridgewater at Yew Tree Farm near Stourbridge, Staffordshire in 1978. Carl was shot in the head at close range while delivering a newspaper to the house. The occupants of the house – elderly cousins Mary Poole and Fred Jones – were not home at the time. Police believed Carl may have disturbed an intruder or burglar, who forced him into the living room and murdered him.

All four men were convicted but in February 1997, after almost two decades of imprisonment and during which time Molloy died, their convictions were overturned on technical grounds and Robinson and Vincent and Michael Hickey were released. Although the crime remains officially unsolved, convicted murderer Hubert Spencer has been mentioned as a possible suspect.

My first job at Gartree was as a machinist in the textile shop but the work was very different from what I was used to. We were making T-shirts and my job was to put the binding round the edges. Each of the boxes contained fifty garments and the weekly task was to complete twenty-six boxes. Upon completion of each box, you recorded it on your timesheet and sent the box to the checking department, who would return any faulty garments for reworking. It wasn't long before I was complaining at how slow my machine was. It was 1,275 revolutions per minute (RPM), which was standard for a clutch motor, but I asked for a faster motor and eventually I was given one that ran at 3,000 RPM. I could complete my twenty-six boxes in a day and a half with this machine.

Although you had to sit at your machine during working hours (with the exception of tea and toilet breaks), once you'd finished the job, the rest of the time was yours to do as you pleased. I tried being idle, but

I soon got bored reading a book, so I turned my attention to working. I set myself a challenge to do as many boxes as I could in a week. I even worked through tea breaks. I believe my record was something like 125 boxes (6,250 garments). If anyone was struggling to complete their task I'd help them out by giving them some of my extra T-shirts – or 'tokens' – to ensure they still earned top money. It was only a few weeks before I had two years' worth of garments tucked in my machine draw. As a result of this I was sometimes asked to fill in on other tasks, such as bar tacking (adding stitches to areas that needed reinforcement) and putting in labels. I stuck at this for a while and then had a brief spell in another workshop packing socks, but this was soul-destroying so I went back to the textile shop until a vacancy became available in the Clothing Exchange Store.

Everything was fine for a while, but it turned sour when the other two inmates and the storeman conspired to have me sacked on the grounds that I was not pulling my weight. It was, however, very much the other way round. I would get the work done so we could sit and relax, whereas they wanted to make the work last all week. Anyway, I was out of there and found myself in the Works Department with the electricians. Unfortunately, I was with another workshy inmate so I fell into a dull daily routine of walking round various parts of the prison looking busy and scrounging cups of tea. I stood it as long as I could and then asked to be placed with the brickies. My request was turned down as there were no vacancies in that area, so I was placed with the painters. However, not being one to let an opportunity pass me by I kept asking if I could work with the brickies. In the end, my wish was granted and Eric became my boss. I forget his surname but occasionally he would tell us stories of the time he spent in Singapore with the Special Boat Service, the navy's equivalent of the SAS. By and large Eric was a private person so it was a rare treat to hear of his overseas adventures. There were two other labourers in our team. I forget their names but they were generous and friendly and we worked well together and were not in the slightest shy of hard graft.

Occasionally, I would go out with Paul, who was uniformed staff at the Works Department and a plumber by trade. In his spare time he played bass guitar in a band made up of other prison staff. He was happy to stay as a trades officer and had no interest in seeking promotion, preferring to get his hands dirty to shuffling papers behind a desk. I enjoyed working with him as he was one of the few members of staff that I could talk to on an equal level. Despite some relaxation in the prison regime, there was still the 'us and them' policy and the feeling of tension that went with it. Staff would put barriers up to keep you in your place and you knew they had the power to discipline you if you stepped out of line. You could never drop your guard and relax as most staff could not be trusted. The trades officers were different as they got close to inmates because they worked with them all day. They saw you as a person not just a number. There was a bond, just like the one you develop with a colleague in any workplace. I felt comfortable working in a team when everyone united for the sake of a common goal. The one downside at Gartree was that inmates had a separate tearoom to the staff. No matter how friendly you became with members of staff, you were always conscious of it being 'us and them'.

For the rest of my time at Gartree I served in the Works Department and I was happy there. During my stay, work was taking place to rebuild and refurbish the wings damaged by the riot. New facilities were being built to make Gartree much bigger, as it was set to become a main centre for lifers in the early assessment stage of their sentence, supplementing the role of Wormwood Scrubs and Wakefield. Eventually, around a third of the inmates would be serving life sentences.

Just as I was feeling settled, time came for another 'career move' and I found myself packing my belongings ready for another transfer. I will give the wing governor his due for keeping his promise to give me fair notice of a transfer as I was told ten months in advance, although I wasn't given the actual date of the move. I had made it clear that I didn't want any surprises like the one I'd got at Wakefield and I was assured that none would be forthcoming. Despite the ten-month warning, they could still tell me to pack the night before, and this was always in the forefront of my mind. As it turned out, I was given about two weeks' notice, which gave me plenty of time to pack and inform my family.

Chapter 7

HMP Maidstone
September 1985-March 1993

As usual, I tried to find out what to expect at Maidstone and I was given various stories. A lot of offenders had passed through its doors, as it is one of the oldest penal institutions in Britain, having been in operation for over 200 years. I certainly got a shock when I arrived at reception. I most certainly was not expecting to see an inmate and maintenance worker driving round on a dumper truck! As I and several others were directed into reception we were offered a cup of tea. Another shock! And it was real tea which made it all the more appreciated. One by one we were called through to another room and our property was checked off. I fully expected to have to empty everything from the boxes and then repack it before going to the wings, but no, they were happy to just accept that you were happy that everything had arrived with you. After answering a few questions about diet, faith and medication and collecting some bedding, our property was loaded on to some barrows and off we went to the wings. The grounds had flower beds dotted about, which was a change from the concrete jungle that most prisons had to offer.

Aerial view of Maidstone Prison.

As we went through the door, I noticed all the railings round the landings were covered in clothes, which were either freshly washed and being left to dry, or dirty and were kept there as the inmates didn't want them in their clean cells. I soon learned that it was a friendly wing and it was relaxed enough that you could leave your belongings lying around, just as you would at home. Even the staff were from a different school of thought. Their policy was you are there *as* punishment not *to be* punished. What a welcome change.

I soon settled in and made friends. Initially I was confronted by those curious to find out where I had come from, what I was in for and how long had I served, but then I became firm friends with three other lifers and together we called ourselves The Four Musketeers. We also gave each other nicknames. Steve Latham was 'The Flying Pig', Allan Cunningham was 'Chrome Dome', Gary Read became 'Garibaldi' and I was 'The Mad Monk'. Steve got his name from the way he would dive for a football while playing in goal and the rest of us were named on account of our receding hairlines.

We were always hanging out together, and in the evenings we'd either watch TV or go into someone's cell and chat. We would also club together and buy ingredients from the prison shop so we could cook a meal together at least once a week. The other three had acquired the status of 'red band', which is when inmates are trusted to take on more responsibility. After completing the Painting and Decorating course, Gary had stayed on as the workshop red band. Allan had served his time on the Bricklaying course and was now the red band for that workshop and Steve held the position of red band in the library. I was working in the carpentry shop but it would be about two years before I got the job of red band. As a red band you got more respect from staff. They would call me by my Christian name rather than 'Downing'. I loved it there. I made a couple of clocks, a TV and video stand for a friend (although he never came to collect it so that was taken home by a member of staff). I also made the flats (scenery) for a play staged in the prison, and the civilian actors who worked with the inmates told me they were better than the flats they had in the theatre. Unfortunately, my spell at the carpentry shop was short lived as once all the contracts had been fulfilled, the shop was cleared of machinery and it was sold to other prisons or put into storage at Branston Stores.

With the workshop now empty, a partition wall was installed with one half donated to the Works Department and the rest made into a 'miscellaneous' workshop, which provided boring, soul-destroying employment. One job involved assembling large plastic daisies on long wire stems. The centres would spin round in the wind, which caused a vibration underground that scared off moles. They were bought largely by the Forestry Commission. We also made plastic weather vanes. I stayed on for a while as the shop red band busying myself with the paperwork but eventually I applied for a job in the print shop. At the time, they didn't have a vacancy for a red band, so they created a post for me. After a few weeks, it was decided part of the shop would be turned into a bookbinding shop and I moved there as the red band and stayed for about a year. Then I saw a vacancy as the Education Department red band and applied. I was instantly turned down by Head of Department Colin Turton, on the grounds that I was not computer literate. I pointed out that everyone had to learn computing at some point in their life as it is not a gift you're born with. My boss also argued in my favour but when that fell on deaf ears, I talked to the deputy governor who immediately accompanied me to the Education Department and informed Colin Turton that, as of Monday, I was the new red band.

I joined the Education Department at the right time as proposals to begin an Office Skills course were starting to take shape. Taught by the female IT instructor, Cherry, the course would have twelve students, take three months and cover all aspects of computing, filing, accounts, spreadsheets and office management. A certificate would be issued to those who had completed the course and achieved a high enough standard to put their skills into practice in the outside world. Cherry was putting the course material together over the six-week summer recess and in order for me to get up to speed with my IT skills I became the guinea pig that tested the course material. I also had to familiarize myself with the work I would be doing for the Education Department.

In the final week of recess, I was joined by Deputy Education Officer Eileen Rowe who gave me information on the new class lists. It was my job to head each list with the class, student's name, the wing they were located on, the tutor who would be taking the class and the location of the classroom. The class lists were designed to allow anyone, especially staff, to locate an inmate quickly and easily. It was also crucial in the event of an emergency evacuation, to check that everyone was accounted for. These lists were issued to all wings, workshops, relevant education staff and security. As the lists were updated every Friday afternoon I would have about two hours to prepare the lists on the computer, adding and subtracting names on each page. Once that was done I could print them off, photocopy the pages, collate and staple them and deliver them to the various locations.

My other job, on Saturday and Sunday mornings, was to see which TV programmes had been requested by inmates and set the two video recorders so they could be taped and then watched at association. All the Open University programmes were recorded, as well as any radio broadcasts, although the latter were dropped once inmates were permitted to have frequency modulation (FM) radios. Originally only radios that had amplitude modulation (AM) and medium wave (MW) were allowed. It was a welcome change as FM offered a wide range of programmes and crystal-clear sound.

In Maidstone, I only watched television two or three hours a week, whereas before I would cabbage in front of the screen every night. They offered evening classes five nights a week here, so I joined a couple with Gary. We enrolled on Domestic Electrical Wiring Installation (it was proposed that a course on Industrial Installation would follow if this course was successful). However, the tutor proved to be a complete arse and most unpopular with the students. The wiring was done in pairs on 8ft by 6ft sheets of 10mm plywood. If there was the slightest kink in the wire, he would go ballistic. We asked him what the problem was, given that during an installation the wire would be fed through a conduit and hidden under plaster, but he said he wanted it to be perfect. Suffice to say student numbers dropped and he was dismissed. It was then announced that the course was too expensive and would not carry on.

Gary and I also joined Drama. Despite making complete fools of ourselves, we kept going as we wanted to see the actress there who had a very gothic style of dress. Both she and the other actors were from the local theatre, although one day they were taken aside and searched by the police after security was tipped off about them bringing drugs in for certain inmates. The drugs were confiscated and they were let off with a caution, although they were never allowed into the prison again, not even under escort.

My other evenings were spent either working in the Education Department, while the evening classes were on, or going to the gym. I would go twice a week, Monday and Thursday, for two hours of weights each session. On Saturday morning I did two hours of circuit training, and in the afternoon, I did two hours' swimming as we had an indoor heated pool, which was 30metres by 10metres. The gym wasn't open on Sunday mornings, but in the afternoon, I'd do an hour on the static bike or lift some weights, followed by an hour in the pool. In all I would train for ten hours a week. Gary preferred to use his Saturday and Sunday afternoons running around the perimeter of the prison. He was a devout Christian so Sunday mornings were spent at the chapel.

Civilians attended the church service alongside the prisoners and although I'm not religious I used to go to meet the visitors and have a cup of coffee with them at the end. Gary had met a woman there called Diane and had asked if he could write to her, but to his disappointment she said she already corresponded with an inmate. However, within a few weeks that correspondence stopped and Diane began to write to Gary. In almost no time at all their friendship turned to love.

They kept it to themselves for as long as they could, but it wasn't long before the chaplain noticed how close they'd become. For security reasons Diane wasn't allowed to come to any more prison church services so she came to see him during the normal visiting hours, just like all the other inmates' loved ones. Now they didn't have to pretend and they could enjoy each other's company. They faced quite a hard time from the chaplain as the psychologist pressured the chaplain into believing that Gary had not told Diane of his offence, but he'd told her every last detail. He couldn't hide it as he had to know if she would be put off, but she wasn't so Gary knew she was the lady for him. Eventually they convinced the two doubters that he'd come clean and they were left alone to enjoy their relationship. Diane waited ten years for Gary to be released and then they married. They are still very happily married and have two wonderful children – a boy and a girl.

Through my friendship with Gary, I got to meet his family, who were very warm, generous and loving. Occasionally we would write to each other and I'd also correspond with Diane. Unfortunately, Gary's father died before he saw his son released. Of the three friends I made in Maidstone, I was closest to Gary and even now we are good friends, although we don't see each other as often as we would like.

Allan was the first to move on. He was very friendly with the wing probation officer and with her help he was granted Category D status. Cat D status is open conditions, so in no time at all we were saying fond farewells to Allan. He had only been in open conditions for about three months when he was eligible for home leave, which is a short period of temporary release. As he didn't have a home to go to, the probation officer invited him to stay with her. We then lost touch because after this, he only corresponded with Gary but added that he wished to be remembered to everyone who knew him.

Steve was the next one to leave although his move wasn't as fortunate as Allan's. He had misread the signs and thought a female civilian librarian with whom he worked was interested in him. He wrote her a letter expressing his feelings, only for her to hand the letter to the prison authorities. Steve was therefore transferred to another prison with higher security. It cost him another five years or so progressing through the system. Nasty rumours circulated, the most damning being that he had attempted to rape her, but this wasn't true and all he was guilty of was writing the letter.

Eventually Gary moved on, although it would be about a year after the others had gone from our little group. In that year, we spent a lot of our leisure time together, watching TV, talking and sharing our hopes and aspirations for the future. One day he showed me some literature he'd got about The Verne Prison in Dorset. Although it was a Cat C establishment it operated almost like a Cat D. It sounded too good to be true and we both set our hearts on going there, but in order to do that we had to be decategorized and that meant convincing the Parole Board that we were trusted enough to progress through the system. From that point on, not one day went by when The Verne didn't come up in our conversation.

The day came when Gary's reports went before the Parole Board. About six weeks later he received its decision – not only had he been granted Cat C status, his request to go to The Verne had also been granted. To say that he was elated is truly an understatement. He bubbled over with joy. While I was happy for him, I was also sad as Gary was the only real mate that I had left. On his final day, I helped him take his property round to reception where we said our fond goodbyes and promised each other that we would stay in touch. True to his word, Gary wrote a few days later and told me all about the place. I was envious that he was able to enjoy the facilities that were on offer, although I would get depressed for a while when he told me he'd been on an escorted town visit and met up with his family, or actually gone home for a while. It did, however, make me all the more determined to follow in his footsteps.

As time moved on, I did consider giving in to the authorities and accepting the guilt in order to get parole and be free. I was conscious that my parents weren't getting any younger and my father had been in poor health having had a heart attack. The thought of being able to visit him – and my mother and sister – at home was never far from my mind. Yet my family would not hear of it and said they weren't giving in and neither should I. They had been campaigning to prove my innocence from day one. Following my arrest, they'd hired a private detective, a retired police officer who discovered that Wendy Sewell had been having several affairs and even had a son out of wedlock who had been adopted. When the press got hold of this, they dubbed her the 'Bakewell Tart' and her colourful love life did add weight to the theory that she'd come to the cemetery to meet a man who wasn't her husband. A man who might have murdered her.

Meanwhile, I made friends with others at Maidstone. I got to know my neighbour in the next-door cell quite well. He introduced himself as Tony Bellchambers and he too was a lifer who had owned a chain of electrical shops around London. That wasn't his first trade though. I was shocked when I heard he was a policeman, until he carried out an armed robbery at a hostel, which earned him a stretch in prison. After release he took up trade as an electrician, but in 1984 he was given a life sentence for organizing a hitman to murder the man with whom his wife was having an affair. He would serve sixteen years before being released in 2000, but three years later he would murder his girlfriend before gassing himself to death in his car.

Tony and I chatted a lot after Gary left and we used to do favours for each other. He worked in the library with Steve (until he was transferred) and he would make sure my book requests were a priority. In return, I'd do his photocopying. He spent most of his time learning the electric piano in his cell, and had reached Level Eight.

Micky Telling was another lifer who worked in the library. Micky was part of the vastly rich Vestey family who founded Dewhurst Butchers. I got on quite well with him, although he was envious if someone had a thing he wanted and would offer them any sum of money to acquire it. He was well off and bought a TV and video recorder for the library so he, Tony and the others could spend the afternoon relaxing in front of the box. I missed out on his generosity when I bought a typewriter from Argos for just under £40 and refused to lend it to him. I explained that he could afford to buy a thousand typewriters but I had very little money and had to look after my belongings, and I went on to question who would replace it if it got broken. I later found out that, had I lent it to him, he would have bought me a laptop for around £2,000. Sure, I missed out, but I believe I was right to stand by my principles and beliefs.

Micky had been married to an American model until he killed her. He'd kept her body in the house for about a month, taking her breakfast each morning and telling her how much he loved her. It was only when the smell got too much that he hacked off her head and placed it in a plastic bag with fishing maggots and disposed of it over a hedge.

Prior to Tony Bellchambers moving in to the cell next to me, it was occupied by Peter Seth-Smith who I got on with exceptionally well. I first got to know him when I bought some handmade leather goods from him. He was truly talented and could turn his hand to just about anything. His hand-tooled leather handbags would sell for between £60 and £250. I bought purses for Christmas presents, which he let me have for £15 instead of £25 as I said that he could have vegetables from my allotment. There were eight allotments in the grounds, which were only available to lifers. I'd had one for about two years and grew lots of fresh produce and salad but I gave quite a lot away as there was far too much for me and I wasn't into cooking now that the rest of the Four Musketeers had moved on to pastures new.

I worked with Peter at the carpentry shop and not only was he first class at woodwork, he was also a qualified silversmith. He was serving time for armed robbery.

One of the *causes célèbres* at Maidstone was the East End gangster Reggie Kray, who had also spent time at Gartree (although our paths never crossed). In May 2015, it was announced that more than 200 letters Kray wrote between 1988 and 1991, when we were both at Maidstone, were to be auctioned for up to £15,000. The letters, sent to the ghostwriter of his autobiography, Carol Clerk, were described as being full of 'bizarre ideas and storylines' for the book. I wonder what my letters would be worth had they been kept! Can't be much worse than Reggie's as, despite the publicity, his letters failed to sell.

I was around ten to twelve years into my sentence before I learned the judge at my trial had set my tariff at seventeen years. At the time, it was customary not to disclose the length of the sentence at conviction, although this was changed some years later. I was not eligible for parole as I was still protesting my innocence, and thus I was not able to show remorse. However, I could be moved to more open conditions.

Around this time, a small number of life-sentence inmates were being given the opportunity to sit in on parole discussion panels and put forward written and verbal representations by a solicitor, paid for by legal aid. At first, I was refused the chance to take part in the trial, but the education officer Colin Turton, the one who had initially dismissed me from working in the IT Department but then saw how hard I'd worked to learn new skills, put forward a strong argument for me to be included. The governor agreed that I should be the last one to take part. Shortly after this trial it became standard practice for life-sentence inmates to sit in on parole hearings, with the results being delivered by a governor-grade officer about two weeks later.

I was anxious for my own parole review so I could enjoy some of the freedoms and pleasures Gary wrote about in his letters. In the meantime, I carried on going to the gym, watching more TV and reading after lock-up. Eventually, my parole review came around and I did all I could to convince staff that they should write their reports in my favour of a transfer to open conditions. Most of the reports were quite favourable, but it was the Parole Board that had the final say. I had to wait the usual six weeks for the answer but it came with the bad news that I would be staying at Maidstone a little longer. The good news was it wanted to review my case again in six months.

By now a pilot scheme was being put into practice where lifers were invited to sit in on the review panel. By the time my reports had been written, all the spaces on the pilot had been filled but again, knowing how disappointed I was not to be a part of it, Colin Turton spoke to the assistant governor who was heading the scheme and again it was agreed that I should be the last one to take part. We met in the boardroom and each member read out their report while I made notes. At the end, I was invited to ask questions, so after consulting my notes I went into attack mode. I put forward my beliefs and theories and questioned the two who were opposed to me being moved to Category C conditions. Having exhausted all my questions and ideas I was sent off back to work.

Fifteen minutes later, Colin arrived back and asked me to make him a cup of coffee. When I took it in, he asked me to close the door and informed me, off the record, that of all the people who had taken part in the pilot scheme, I was the only one that had asked the right questions and I had come across as the most literate. The two that had been against my move to Cat C had changed their minds and were now in favour of the move. I was delighted. With the entire panel behind me, I knew I must have a better chance of the Parole Board granting me the move.

Just two weeks after my reports were sent off, I was called to the office and told that my Parole Board answer was back. My heart sank as it had been such a short period of time, I was sure it must be bad news. But no, to my relief, I was told I had been granted Cat C status and the Home Office was also in favour of me being transferred to The Verne. I was overjoyed at the news and had to tell my family straight away.

On average, a lifer spends two to four years in a single establishment. I'd served seven in Maidstone. I spent the first six years in the Medway Wing but it had got very rowdy with a large influx of younger prisoners serving short fixed sentences. Tony Bellchambers and I had wanted some peace and quiet and applied to move to the Wield Wing, which was much calmer.

My transfer date was set for 12 March, so I prepared a last meal for Tony, Micky and another friend whose name escapes me. Ever since the days of the Four Musketeers, it had been custom (for us four) to prepare a meal for a friend's birthday. As I'd had my birthday on 4 March, it was a double celebration.

Chapter 8

HMP The Verne
March 1993-November 1994

HMP The Verne is a Category C prison located within the nineteenth century Verne Citadel, on the Isle of Portland in Dorset. Built to defend Portland Harbour, the citadel housed the Royal Engineers until 1948 and the following year, the southern part of the citadel was made into a prison. The first twenty inmates arrived on 1 February 1949 and since then, its interior has been rebuilt substantially by prison labour. It would be like nothing I'd experienced before.

On 12 March, I was up early to finish my packing before waiting to be called to reception. After having my property checked I climbed on the coach and headed off to HM Young Offenders' Institution Feltham where I was to transfer to another coach. Once we arrived at Feltham I was given some lunch and told that I would be spending the night at HMP Winson Green, Birmingham. This was a blow. I'd hated the place twenty

The Verne with its spacious grounds, which inmates were free to roam.

plus years previously, when I spent one week there while transferring between prisons, and I doubted it had changed for the better. I was right. Apart from the installation of sanitation, it was no different and was still a stinking cesspit. Thank God it was only for one night.

The next morning, I climbed aboard the waiting coach and again headed off for Feltham where I was, again, given lunch. However, it transpired that we had arrived late and missed the coach going to The Verne! Arrangements were made for me to get to HMP Wandsworth for the night – another hellhole. Still it was only for one night. At least that was what I was told but on arrival, when I asked if I would be going to The Verne the next day, Wednesday, the SO laughed and told me there was only one pick-up a week for The Verne and that was the following Tuesday.

That week dragged like a year. The meals were swill that I would be ashamed to serve to pigs and the accommodation was a festering pit of filth. The only thing I can say in its favour is that the wing staff were marginally friendlier than the animals working in reception. Eventually, the day came when I was heading for reception and again on the coach to Feltham. After yet another lunch there, I finally boarded the coach for The Verne. Immediately, I noticed a huge change in the attitude of the staff compared to the people I'd met over the past couple of weeks. They were quick to have a conversation and share a few laughs with us. On the way, we had to stop as a Land Rover was blocking the road and while we all volunteered to get off and push it to the side of the road, it was the staff who got off to assist the driver.

It was just as relaxed when I got to The Verne. After being ushered into reception, we were given cups of tea and offered a meal while staff unloaded our property for us. One by one we were called through to the reception desk to have our property checked off. Without leaving me to wait, the reception orderlies then helped load up a barrow, showed me to the wing and introduced me to the officer there. Then I was given a key and shown to my room. Room. Not cell. You had your own door key, staff had a master key and you were never locked up at night. As the toilets and bathrooms were out on the landing, you could use them throughout the night, otherwise you were not supposed to leave your room after 11.00 pm without good reason. The window consisted of a huge, 4ft square pane of glass and there was a small window to the side that could be opened. There were no bars. There was also a radiator, which I could control so the temperature was to my taste.

Unless you were at work, you were free to roam the grounds from 8.00 am until 9.00 pm. From time to time, a siren would sound and everyone would be expected to come in and stand by their door for a roll check. After you'd finished work, and at lunch and dinnertime, a member of staff would stand at the door and tick you off as you came in. The outside doors would remain locked until everyone had been accounted for, which usually took about fifteen minutes. You could either eat in the dining room or take food into your own room. There was a large TV room, a ping pong table in the hallway and a dartboard in the dining room. There were also several table games that could be borrowed from the office. Each wing also had a card phone, although you could go on to another wing and use theirs, providing a resident from that wing wasn't using it.

By and large we were left to our own devices with very little staff activity and in return, there was very little disturbance from the inmates. Most of the time, staff relied on radio contact. It wasn't unheard of for just one member of staff to look after two wings, when previous establishments would require ten or twelve staff to man a wing before they even considered unlock. The level of trust was exceedingly high and the 600 or so inmates respected that. Over the years I came to realize that small prisons allowed for a better rapport between inmates and staff, which meant there was less unrest. Rather than 'us and them', each side respected the other and their role in the prison. I don't know what the statistics are but I bet fewer inmates in a prison this size return to crime compared to one the size of the Scrubs, which is home to around 2,500 men.

Des, the reception orderly who had walked me down to the wing, had identified me the moment I walked in as Gary must have mentioned me. I was really looking forward to seeing Gary but he was at work until 4.30 pm so Des showed me where he sat in the dining room and I sat at the same table and waited for him. However, when Gary arrived he said I was in someone's seat so I moved to another chair but he said that was taken too. I was disappointed that he hadn't bothered to save me a place, which is something mates usually do. He did say there were free places at some of the other tables, but I said I would eat in my room, which is what I did throughout my whole stay there. Even when spaces became available, I was never invited to join them although Gary and I used to take a walk together after meals. He'd got in with the wrong crowd, which I did tell him at the time. I was proved right when, after being released, one of his good friends, Claude, took a woman hostage and raped her repeatedly.

Gary was on the Painting and Decorating course when I arrived, but left to join me in the Education Department so we could both do a short Business Studies course under the tutelage of Edmund Fisher. We had a laugh at his expense when it emerged that he was doing the accounts for the family grocery store, which went bankrupt, before setting up his own business, which also went bankrupt and that's why he began teaching Business Studies at The Verne.

Fisher decided that we should operate a business selling greeting cards. The venture was set up with a £100 loan from the governor. In order to make it a success, there had to be a decent range of cards on offer and they had to be cheaper than the cards on sale in the canteen (the prison shop). We had lots of ideas for the type of cards we wanted to sell but Fisher wasn't prepared to listen to us and stocked up on the designs he liked. He, of course, took care of all the sales. Our job was simply to put the word out and tell others that they were on sale. The downside was that you couldn't have the cards until the money had been deducted from your earnings. Of course, when people heard how the scheme worked, they didn't want to know and they were prepared to pay that little bit more and buy from the canteen. I was in the same frame of mind although I did buy one from Fisher. Needless to say, within a few weeks that 'business' went bust – racking up a hat trick for Fisher – and the governor wasn't best pleased to lose the money he'd borrowed from prison funds.

As I was nearing the end of the course, a vacancy arose for the post of education orderly so I applied and at interview explained that I was able to do any computing that was needed as well as all the spreadsheets, having done them for three years at Maidstone. I assured them that I would be given a good report from staff there, if they wished to check up. I got the job.

My role was to open files for the newcomers and close files when an inmate was transferred. I added information such as name, age, date of birth, religion, where they had been transferred from, length of sentence and previous educational studies. Occasionally I would be told a person's offence, although I couldn't care less what anyone was in for. Anyone discharged had their file sent to admin who forwarded it to the Home Office to be filed in the archives.

After about ten months I left to work in the kitchen. I made the move after learning that the two orderlies working in the computer suite and in the pottery classroom had been given a £1-a-week pay increase for doing far less than me. When my request for a pay rise was refused, even with staff backing my claim, I left the £6-a-week job as an education orderly to join the bakers on £9.40 a week. It was an early start as the hours were 6.00 to 10.00 am every day and overtime of 2.00 to 4.30 pm twice a week.

To begin with there were three of us baking until one got the sack but then Tim, my fellow baker, and I were able to do the job well enough between us and we got a pay rise that took us to £11.90 basic and £13.50 with overtime. At first we wore orderly jackets but health and safety regulations changed and we had to wear proper chefs' jackets (even though they were made from the same material as the orderly jackets). It wasn't long before I learned all the fiddles. Working in the kitchen meant we had access to yeast, a valuable commodity in any prison as it is used for brewing hooch. A bag of yeast – amounting to about a teaspoonful – would exchange hands for a £2 phone card and be enough to brew a 9-litre bucket. The idea was you paid for the yeast and then when you'd brewed the hooch, you'd sell a 2-litre bottle for a phone card. Seven litres was more than enough for eight to ten people to have an enjoyable Friday and Saturday night. Very few drank on a Sunday as they didn't want to feel rough at work the next day and didn't want to make staff suspicious by brandishing a very obvious hangover. Tim and I worked well together and I enjoyed the work very much, far more than I had in the Education Department.

Despite this, I was depressed. After years of being locked up, I was struggling to cope with the amount of autonomy I was given at The Verne. I told Gary I was going to ask for a move to closed conditions. I was sure I'd be able to handle anything that was thrown at me. But Gary persuaded me to stay and I'm jolly glad that he did as, not only would I would have missed out on a continued friendship, but I have some wonderful memories of a two-day home visit and spending a few hours with my family on town visits when they came to Weymouth for the week. As my family lived far away and couldn't visit regularly, I would save up my visits and they would come down for a week and then they'd visit me every day and on one of the days we'd go to town.

To qualify for a home or town visit, you had to be within a year of a parole review, and then you could apply to have either a home or town visit every three months. I was jealous of Gary who was already enjoying time out and was also getting extra trips out courtesy of one of the POs he was friendly with. I'm a big believer in fairness and felt very strongly that one person should not be treated better than another and it's a policy I still hold to this day. But, sadly, that is the nature of the beast when it comes to prison survival. The stronger, wilier types will win more than the weaker men. That is until the weaker inmates clamber up to their level.

It wasn't long before I also found myself in a good position. Just like at Maidstone, I became friendly with the staff and could acquire things in return for doing them favours. I may not have had as many trips out of the prison as Gary, but I knew others were envious of me. I seemed to be liked by all the staff, which was later reflected in a report that would be sent to the Parole Board.

In order to have a town visit, accompanied by your case officer in plain clothes, you needed to save up a minimum of £10 from your earnings and up to £15 of your private cash. The prison also gave you £15 to buy a meal and drinks. I saved as much as I could for these days out, and once I was able to take £135 with me. Family and friends were also permitted to meet up with you at the Home Office's discretion and they were allowed to spend money on you. Officially you were only supposed to bring back items that were on the 'approved privileges' list, but occasionally your case officer would be happy to bring other items in for you. The first time I went out on a home visit, it extended to two days because the journey took more than five hours to get to the family home. I spent the night in Nottingham Prison before returning to see my family for a few hours.

During my time at The Verne, a project called the 'Listener scheme' was introduced. Listeners would be inmates trained and supported by counsellors from the local branch of the Samaritans, who would themselves visit the prison every fortnight so inmates could talk to them confidentially. I have always been keen to help others so I volunteered for training. I was able to get time off from work in the kitchen for the six two-hour training sessions over a six-week period. At the end of the training, we were issued a badge so that we could be identified.

It wasn't long before I was approached by an inmate who asked if he could talk to me in confidence. I assured him that he could and he told me that he had been making obscene telephone calls. He was sorry about what he'd done and asked if I would apologize to the person concerned on his behalf. I said that I would. He said her name was Judith and she worked in probation.

After three or four failed trips to probation, I found her and asked if I could talk to her. She told me my probation officer was in his office. I said that I was there as part of the Listener scheme and she invited me into her office. I explained that the nature of my business made me feel uncomfortable but she assured me I should just come straight out with it. I began by asking if she'd received any obscene phone calls and she told me she had. I then went on to tell her what my client had told me the night before. Judith asked me who it was, but I reminded her that I was bound by confidentiality and was only passing on the apology as requested. She thanked me for coming to see her and asked if I minded if she spoke to her boss about it. I said it was fine with me.

That night, half an hour after the evening meal, I was called to the wing office and was told that Senior Probation Officer Steven Leadley would like to see me. He wasted no time in informing me that Judith Hartsilver had been to see him and repeated everything I'd told her earlier that day. I confirmed that it was true. He asked me who had made the calls, but I told him that I was bound by the confidentiality of the Samaritans policy. He was far from happy and started to threaten me with prosecution. I was in no mood to be threatened and said he would have to do what he felt was right. He asked if I would be willing to ask the inmate if he would come forward and report back the following morning. I said I'd do my best.

Thinking I was possibly being spied on by staff, I chatted with a number of inmates to confuse anyone that was watching. The inmate in question said he was too ashamed to come forward and that he was sorry for his actions and the distress it had caused. I reported to Leadley as promised and said I'd spoken with the inmate but he was not willing to come forward and I was still duty bound not to disclose his identity. I also told him two of the Samaritans were going to come and see me later that day. I had phoned them the night before.

I met with the Samaritans and explained everything. They asked a few questions including whether I knew the contents of the alleged telephone calls. I didn't as I hadn't asked. After about an hour and a half they said that they were happy with the way I had handled the situation and would speak with the governor. I never heard from them again.

The following day I went to work and all was normal until security came in to the kitchen and said that they were taking me for a room search. I had nothing to hide and therefore had nothing to worry about. Room searches seldom happened in The Verne and as I hadn't given anyone cause to warrant a search, I could only deduce that Leadley was seeking some kind of revenge. Throughout the course of the search one of the two members of staff kept asking the other if he could consult a small piece of pink paper. At the end they told me that they would be taking away a number of items, including my diary. I said that I would require a receipt and they said they'd see what they could do. I was then allowed to return to work. One of the uniformed kitchen staff asked me what the search was for – I said I didn't know and explained my theory and told him items had been taken away. He agreed that it was probably instigated by Leadley and said that he was a nasty piece of work. He was adamant I needed a receipt and I assured him that I'd asked for one. I remember thinking it was a strange reaction from a member of staff and sometimes I wonder if I should have asked him why he was on 'my side'.

Word got round and the staff I spoke to were shocked that I was being targeted. I told the Samaritans of the search and asked if there was any feedback from their visit with the governor. I was told that there wasn't, other than that he was dealing with the matter. I asked if I should tell any staff members the name of my client and was told I should. I informed my case officer, Peter Melnyk, who said that I should tell the lifer governor, Clive Tanner. However, he wasn't around so I had to see Mr Bunning, the lifer PO. I explained the situation and disclosed the client's name. He said that he would probably see Tanner at lunch and would pass on the information.

I was never criticized for the way I handled the situation but, despite my efforts to help my fellow inmates, the prison governors decided that it was me who had to carry the can for the whole matter. It came to a head when I was called to the office after work in the morning and informed by Tanner that I should pack my belongings as I would be transferred to HMP Dorchester at 2.00 pm. I looked at my watch. It gave me two hours to pack everything and I also had to inform my family as they were planning to visit me shortly. After several failed attempts to contact them, I decided to leave it a while and start packing. First I had to locate some boxes so I went to reception but there was no one there. This really was a great start. I got back to the wing and again tried calling home without success. Why was all this happening to me? Twenty-two years into my sentence and this is what I get for trying to help others. It was certainly not going to bode well with the Parole Board. I was due to begin interviews in about six months. I never looked forward to them at the best of times and I knew that I was going to be under even more pressure than normal, and I was right. I did eventually manage to contact my parents and deliver the bitter pill but with my diary taken away in the search, I wasn't able to call my sister at work as I couldn't remember the number. Nor could I remember my father's mobile number, hence I had to keep trying the home phone.

I managed to acquire enough boxes and with the help of staff and other inmates I packed all my belongings. Even the wing staff tried to reason with Tanner and see if the transfer could be put off until the following day, but he was having none of it. Eventually, I was told the move was only for three weeks while the matter was being investigated and then I would be moving back to The Verne. Personally, that seemed ludicrous, but if that is what it would take then so be it. It would be several weeks before I learned it was a ploy on behalf of Head of Custody Governor Bowkett to have me permanently transferred out of The Verne. However, I had my wits about me and decided it would be wise to get myself a solicitor.

I contacted the firm Humphries Kirk in Dorchester as it was only a few minutes' walk from the prison and Simon Lacey was the solicitor appointed to my case. I was extremely pleased with his work as he certainly gave Dorset Police a run for their money. Despite their investigations all they could say were that the calls were traced to B Wing. Yes I lived on that wing but so did many others, and inmates were also permitted to use phones on other wings. Almost 600 inmates had access to the wing payphones. If the police or the prison authorities were as vigilant as they claimed, they only had to check with the canteen to see how many phone cards I bought and then look at the phone company records to see how often I made calls and for what duration. They would soon discover I used the majority of the cards to call my family. I would call on a Saturday and a Sunday and use a full £2 card on each occasion and ring a couple of times in the week with a third card. A £2 phone card gave you about ten minutes at the weekend and seven minutes during the week. Twenty-seven minutes cost £6 and at the time I was earning, with overtime, only around £14 a week. I certainly didn't have money to waste on any other kind of calls. After all I was not getting fortnightly visits anymore, so my only contact with family was via letter or phone call and there is nothing more pleasing or satisfying than to hear a loved one's voice at the other end of the phone.

I also found out some time later that the calls were made around 10.00 pm. If that was the case, it could only have been a member of staff as the phones were turned off for inmates at 9.00 pm. Anyway, why would another inmate come to me and admit to making inappropriate calls? The only explanation was that staff had conspired to blame me and have me transferred, but that idea seemed too far-fetched, not to mention complicated. If they wanted me out that badly, the governor only needed to contact the Lifer Management Unit (LMU) at the Home Office and make a request for my transfer by offering a far simpler reason. Lifers can only be transferred with the approval of the LMU.

When it became obvious that I did not have access to the particular phone from which the obscene calls were made, and that I would have been in my cell at the time they were made, the inquiry against me was suddenly dropped and I never received any explanation or apology. Despite this, Simon Lacey's efforts to get me back to The Verne were in vain as the Home Office refused to sanction the move.

During my time in The Verne, I decided not enough was being done to fight my case so I contacted Paul Dickinson, the solicitor who had recommended I be remanded rather than bailed all those years ago, to see what was happening. I explained that I wanted to look into my case and would be most grateful if he could send me any papers he might have. Around a month later, I received a large envelope with a covering letter to say that he had sent all the papers he was able to find and apologized for not having the time to check through any of them. I thanked him for his time and effort and said I was delighted with what he had sent. I now had all the original trial statements, scenes of crime photos, photos from the hospital and mortuary as well as maps of the cemetery.

Home visit with Mum.

With school friend Richard Brailsford and Mum and Dad.

Left: With Mum and Dad and prison officer Andy Fear.

Right: Another anniversary I missed: Mum and Dad's 40th, September 1994.

Without wasting any time, I read the statements and jotted down notes. When I finished I read them again and again, making more notes each time until I had 112 pages of them. I tried to answer as many of my own questions as I could and to find logic and reasoning in what I considered to be flaws. Why, I wondered, had no one else picked up on them? And if they had why were they not highlighted? I was baffled as to why the defence counsel hadn't found them, or if they had, why they hadn't challenged them. There was a lot to work on but for now, everything would have to be put on hold to accommodate this unexpected transfer from The Verne.

Chapter 9

HMP Dorchester
November 1994-June 1996

Having arrived at Dorchester, I was shown into a dark and dingy area of reception to wait processing. Even though I was the only person there, I was left for around three hours before I was dealt with. Nevertheless, I found the staff friendly enough and I was offered a cup of tea, which helped warm me up for a while. I was told that most of my property – which amounted to ten boxes – would be kept in reception but I could take what I needed for the night. I settled for toiletries and my radio. Eventually I was led to the wing, where I was informed that I wouldn't be able to keep any phone cards and all my calls would be monitored. I was not happy about this as it felt like an infringement of the few rights I had in prison and I hadn't been found guilty of any offence. But, of course, phone calls are not a right but a privilege that can be taken away as punishment, even if you are being penalized unfairly. It was also a huge inconvenience as often I would have to wait for lengthy periods to get a card from the office, which meant that I missed getting into the queue early and would find myself behind fifty or more waiting to use one of the two phones.

Dorchester Prison, which was a typical Victorian design.

Dorchester is a rather small prison housing around 350 inmates, mostly two to a cell. As a lifer, I was given a cell to myself although Gerry, the wing-cleaning officer, said that I may have to share if they became overcrowded. Fortunately for me, it was never the case. I got on with Gerry and he would leave me unlocked as long as I didn't wander off the landing. He also said he'd give me a bit of cleaning to do as and when it became available. If Gerry wasn't on duty, I wasn't unlocked.

The morning after my arrival, I asked Gerry to take me to reception so I could go through my belongings. I put everything I wanted to one side and disposed of magazines and papers that were of no use to me. Anything I wanted destroyed had to be taken off my property cards and signed for by myself in the presence of the reception office. Things I wanted to take up to my cell also had to be noted on my property cards. I made sure I had my typewriter, all the case documents and my notes, and over the next few weeks I made several trips to reception to acquire various items of property. Once it was established that I would be staying at Dorchester for a while, I was asked to sort out my belongings to reduce the number of boxes being stored as the new prison rule, laid out by the Home Office, was that only two boxes were permitted, plus one large item. However, as I was a lifer, it was expected that I would accumulate things over the years, so they made an exception for me and told me to reduce the volume to an acceptable level. If I couldn't, I'd have to hand stuff to my family when they visited or have it sent to Branston Stores, which meant I wouldn't be able to access it for twelve months. It was rather a tight squeeze but I managed to get it all down to five boxes, and reception said they'd do their best to store it.

The Verne was seen as a relatively fast track establishment aimed towards release. A lifer might serve two or three years there before virtually being guaranteed a move to open conditions where, after perhaps a further two years, they should be ready to be released on licence. After moving to The Verne, I was looking to be out on licence within five years and this gave me and my family a glimmer of light at the end of the never-ending tunnel. Now with a blot on my otherwise perfect copybook, I was going to have to re-evaluate my position and consider what effect it had on my future.

I tried finding out what I could from the Samaritans when they visited Dorchester. However, I only got as far as waving to them before being informed the Samaritans were only able to see unconvicted inmates! If anyone on the convicted wing wanted an audience with a Samaritan, they were placed on suicide watch and a self-harm register was opened. Even when I explained my reasons for requesting a meeting with a Samaritan, and insisting that I was not suicidal and nor was I intent on self-harm, I was told they couldn't take any chances. I was on the register for about a month. Officially, no record of being on the register should be kept on your file, although I suspect that isn't the case.

I hadn't been at Dorchester long, when interviews began for my Parole Board hearing. Most would be carried out by staff at Dorchester, but psychiatrists and psychologists had to come in from outside. I was horrified when I found out that the person writing my psychology report was Julia Long. She was the prison psychologist at The Verne and hadn't liked me from the moment we met as I wasn't prepared to admit to the offence. She made it abundantly clear that she would not write anything favourable about me until I was prepared to accept my guilt for the crime. She was in for a very long wait. I had stood by my convictions for all these years and I was not about to give in now, just to put a feather in her cap.

She made it clear that she would be writing a very negative report and I could never expect to be released after what I had done. I asked her what she meant and she said making the obscene phone calls and frightening that poor woman. I was shocked and made no attempt to disguise my anger. I told her she could write whatever she wanted on the report. I really did not give a damn if I got out or not as I was not going to throw in the towel for anyone.

The psychiatrist was Dr Rowton-Lee, whom I had met previously when he wrote a glowing report in favour of me moving to open conditions; he felt there was nothing to gain by keeping me locked up and I would only stagnate further. I wondered what his report would say this time. At interview it seemed he was still of the same mindset and implied his report would reflect that. I was relieved that I could count on one positive report to counter that of the vindictiveness of Julia Long's. She even went so far as to send a second report to the Home Office and Parole Board and added that she had spoken with her colleague, Judith Hartsilver, who asked her to amend her report to say that she was not frightened of me but terrified. My solicitor and I could not believe Julia had actually amended her report on someone else's say so. At the parole hearing, it was pointed out that the amendment should be inadmissible on the grounds that it was Judith Hartsilver who wanted the change made. Despite this, the Parole Board accepted the addendum on the grounds that Julia Long was permitted to add to her report and consult with her colleague.

I had made one foolish and fatal mistake while at The Verne, and that was to ask the receptionist at my trial solicitor's firm if I might correspond with her. She said no but said I could call her, which I did on no more than four occasions, with each conversation only lasting a few minutes. It was on the final call that she asked me not to call her again and I respected her wishes. I don't know how the authorities got to know of these calls, but it seems she too was now making out that they were obscene and, furthermore, so was Eileen Rowe from the Education Department at Maidstone Prison, with whom I'd worked for three years. I had said that I would call and let her, as well as several other members of staff, know when I had arrived at my new establishment and other than that we exchanged a few letters which petered out after four or five. That is the only contact I had with her after I had left.

It was clear that the governors at The Verne were spoiling for a dirty fight. As is the norm in a situation that involves a lifer, he or she will always come off worse. I was devastated to find out that people I'd worked with so closely were being persuaded to make false and malicious allegations against me. I was also baffled as to why they were allowing themselves to be manipulated in this way. What did they stand to gain from it? Anyone who has had the misfortune to go up against the authorities will know only too well that Joe Bloggs stands a snowball in hell's chance of winning.

By the end of my third week at Dorchester, the investigation was completed, so I expected to return to The Verne within a few days. By the end of the fourth week, and with no sign of moving, I made enquiries and was told I would be there for another two weeks as they didn't have any vacancies. At least I had a timescale to work to and I informed my family of the imminent move. Like me they were delighted as we could look forward to even more town and home visits, given that I was within a year of my parole hearing. In my second month at Dorchester, I learned that I would not be going back to The Verne. Despite not having a scrap of evidence to support any of these claims or allegations, the Home Office ruled that I should remain at Dorchester, a local prison that did not have the staff or the facilities to cater for lifers. In the end, I was kept at Dorchester for twenty months, before being moved to Dartmoor for additional psychology reports.

While I was at Dorchester, Don Hale, the former editor of the *Matlock Mercury,* wrote to me asking if I would outline the events from that day in 1973 up to the present. I was pleased that someone was taking an interest in my case and wasted little time putting it all down on paper. I was so keen to have as much information passed on to Don that when I finished a week later, I'd completed eighty pages. He wrote back to thank me and say that there was far more than he had ever expected.

It was my father who had made telephone contact with Don Hale in September 1994. He'd outlined my case and the fact that I was still in prison after almost twenty-one years for a murder I did not commit. A face to face appointment was arranged for 2.30 pm, which both Mum and Dad attended. With all the facts in his possession, Don agreed to take on my miscarriage of justice case. This was to be the start of many meetings between the three, which would culminate, some six years later, in my release from prison and a successful appeal against conviction. It would be a long, heavy slog to reach that point.

Don set about reading the large bundle of paperwork from the 1974 appeal file and went through it with a fine-tooth comb. I won't go into this at length but refer the reader to Don's 2002 book *Town Without Pity*, in which he details the finer points of my case. In December 1994, Don presented a portfolio of evidence to the then Chief Constable of Derbyshire Constabulary John Newing, to the Home Office and to the local MP Patrick McLoughlin. On 26 December, I wrote Don a letter from HMP Dorchester, of which this is an extract:

> 'Dear Don, I would like to say thank you to you and your staff for taking an interest in my case, but above all for believing in my innocence. I appreciate that it is quite an undertaking for a small paper to take on, also in view of its limited number of readers. I hope that I am able to help you with your investigation as much as I possibly can. I trust that what I have sent will be enough to get you started. Stephen Downing.'

From January 1995, and throughout that year, Don followed up every single point I had made in the thick file of notes I'd sent him, and on 27 January he published the first of many articles about my case in the *Matlock Mercury*. At the end of January, Patrick McLoughlin,

MP for West Derbyshire, presented Don's first submission to the Home Office and Don personally delivered Chief Constable Newing's copy, which was thirty pages long. The main headings were as follows: the method of interrogation constituted oppression; the contents of Stephen Downing's confession, which he later retracted, do not fit the known facts; the forensic evidence, the timings, the scene of crime procedures, the new witness statements and other considerations.

I sent Don a letter:

'Dear Don, Thanks for sending the copies of the proposed submission. I have read it several times so that I am familiar with the contents. It puts across a strong argument to support and uphold my claim of innocence. Hoping that your time-honoured efforts will not have been in vain. Best regards, Stephen Downing.'

In February 1995, the *Daily Star* became the first national newspaper to take up my cause when it published an article with the headline: '22 Years In Jail – But Is He Innocent?' and a few days later, it carried another full-page article about my case. On 15 February, I wrote to Don:

'It really is amazing the power the press has on people... . I find it equally hard to believe that the police have allowed vital evidence to remain in a vault for almost 22 years. It seems that they were desperate to secure a conviction and a fast one, with little regard for who shouldered the blame. It has often been said that the truth will always prevail and it now looks as if I am on the path that proves, yet again, the adage is true... . The wealth of evidence contained in the dossier would appear to offer the Home Secretary little choice in what action he can take... . Stephen Downing.'

Time was dragging and with every letter I received or phone call I made, I hoped desperately for more news and further progress. My family told me things were happening in the background and I tortured them with my demanding questions. Perhaps they only knew as much as I did, but inside it felt as though I was being kept in the dark, as if no one trusted me. Why didn't they want to tell me the latest developments? Surely this was an exciting time for all of us. All I could do was hang in there and hope that news would reach me sooner rather than later.

My memory is sketchy now, but I guess a few weeks went by, perhaps a couple of months, before I was told Don had enlisted the help of a medium to shed some light on the events that fateful day. I was surprised at this and thought immediately of the little old lady in the *Poltergeist* films. Don had a copy of the *Mercury* sent to me each week and I looked forward to the next instalment, especially with this latest revelation, which I was sure was going to attract mega sales. The paper would usually arrive on a Friday, occasionally on a Saturday. As soon as I collected it from the wing office, I would dash to my cell and frantically tear off the wrapper and, having whipped myself up into a frenzy, begin flicking through the pages in an effort to find any related article. This time, I was in such a rush that I missed the story. Calming myself down, I went through the paper again until I found what I was looking for. The medium said Wendy Sewell had been attacked in one place and moved to another and had been choked, perhaps with a pair of tights. She also said I was innocent and gave the initials of the man she claimed was the murderer. But what really drew my attention was that when I looked at the medium's picture, I knew it was no little old lady. Although she had her back to the camera it was easy to see that she was quite young with a fabulous figure and stunning legs – certainly nothing like the medium in the *Poltergeist* films.

The paper gave her name only as Christine and when I called my family I asked for her surname. At first, they said they didn't know and then later they admitted that they were not able to say, for her protection. I responded by saying that I wasn't likely to do her any harm and eventually my father said: 'You'll never guess what it is.' I took a stab in the dark and said 'Smith?' Turns out I was right.

I had to find out more about her. I was sure that someone that beautiful must be married or have a boyfriend. During a family phone call, I asked my mother where Christine lived and she said Chesterfield. I asked for the address so I could write and thank her for getting involved, but she didn't have it. I was devastated. Shortly after, I heard that Christine was unwell with a bad cold so I bought a get-well card from the canteen, enclosed a brief letter and sent it to Don to pass on. It was about three weeks before I got a reply. Christine had put her address and phone number on her letter so I gave her a call and we had a lengthy chat lasting the whole of my phone card. I also wrote a letter that night saying how wonderful it was to talk with her. We started to correspond with each other and after a while, I asked if she would send me a photo so I could see what she looked like. She said she was ugly and had a big hairy wart on her nose but I persisted and she gave in. A couple of weeks went by until a bulky envelope arrived with a twelve-page letter and six wonderful photos. I laid them out in front of me and stared at them. Wow! I couldn't believe how beautiful she was and how lucky I was to be writing to her. This only ever happened to other people. I was worried that I'd wake up and find that it had all been a dream.

I must have looked at those pictures for well over an hour and only became aware of the time when I heard my cell door being unlocked for afternoon work. That afternoon, I kept returning to my cell to look at them and I got a warm glow inside when I thought she was only at the end of a letter or a phone line. For a while I kept them in the envelope, not daring to put them up on my picture board knowing that photographs were prone to being stolen. Eventually, I did put them up. I was proud to display them and even more proud when others asked who she was and commented on her beauty. With each letter and phone call I shared with Christine, I couldn't stop gushing about how beautiful she was. We were becoming increasingly close and I told her repeatedly that I loved her. I longed to spend hour after hour chatting with her, but that would have to wait, although for how long would be anyone's guess.

Christine would often tell me about the readings she did for people, and the exorcisms she carried out, although she never revealed the identity of her clients. I told her I was interested in the paranormal and read many books on the subject providing that it was a work of fact rather than fiction from the hands of someone like Stephen King. I said that when I was released I'd like to video her working on an exorcism. At first she wasn't too keen but then she warmed to the idea. It sounds daft – here I was making all these plans for the future, a future I so desperately wanted to spend with Christine, but I didn't even know when I was getting out. *If* I was getting out.

Despite having never met her, one Saturday morning three months after we started our correspondence, I got down on one knee in front of the whole wing and asked her to marry me over the phone. My heart fell to the floor when she said she was flattered but she didn't think her boyfriend Rick would like it. She hadn't mentioned a boyfriend before and she knew how hurt I was. She tried to laugh it off, saying I didn't know her and she didn't know me, but I knew Christine well enough to want her to say yes and for me to spend the rest of my life with her.

A few weeks later she wrote to tell me her boyfriend had walked out on her (again) following a big argument but this time she wasn't having him back. She went on to say that Rick was practising satanic witchcraft but didn't go into detail. Towards the end of her letter she wrote: 'I am sure, like you say, destiny will bring us together one day. Like you say it is just a matter of time.' She signed off with a kiss and I was over the moon as I felt as though I'd won her over.

Christine had a daughter, Sally, who at that time was about 14 or 15 and was still at school. I was delighted to receive a letter from her, as it was more correspondence to look forward to. I enjoyed reading about how well she was doing at school and listening to her teenage problems. I wanted Sally to be the daughter I'd always longed to have; someone I could dote on and be proud of. However, after a couple of letters and a postcard, she stopped writing although I still received news of Sally via her mum, which was nice.

When I found out I wouldn't be transferring back to The Verne, I was told I'd be getting a transfer to somewhere else as the Dorchester was not geared to accommodate lifers. I asked where I'd be going and was told they didn't know as it was for the LMU at the Home Office to make the decision. I said it would be most appreciated if they would give me some notice and not just spring it on me the night before, or even a few hours before, as The Verne had done. They assured me they would, although I was sceptical. Virtually every week I was in the office asking about a move as I wanted to be sure of plenty of notice. Then I got word I was on the move, but no date or place. Eventually I was given a date and, as promised, I had about six weeks to organize myself. While at Dorchester I had another unsuccessful parole review, the outcome of which meant it would be another two years before the next review. This was a bitter disappointment for me and my family but, looking on the bright side, two years was not as bad as it could have been. Eventually, I was given a date of transfer and informed that I would be going to Dartmoor for further assessment.

Chapter 10

HMP Dartmoor
June 1996-January 1997

I'd heard grim tales about Dartmoor and absolutely dreaded going. I can say, without hesitation or prejudice, that Dartmoor really does live up to its reputation. I went there in June and it was cold and it would only get colder. I did make friends though. Across the landing was a fellow lifer called Winston. He had turned to writing and was in the process of penning a hefty tome about the history of prison from the sixteenth century to the present day. The Home Office was supplying him with historical documents and hundreds of photographs from the archives. He also had his work published in several magazines, and when I discovered he was being paid for his articles I decided to follow suit. I wrote several articles and short stories, which I then mailed off to different magazines, but sadly they all came back with rejection slips. Winston reassured me that rejection was normal. He'd had quite a few until one piece got published and then he seemed to be accepted more than he was rejected. He'd had a science fiction book published too, although it hadn't done too well.

When the cell to my right became vacant, Winston moved in and before long we were the best of friends. This was a comfort because I was even further away from home than The Verne so I didn't have any visits and had to contend myself with letters and phone calls. I wasn't working so I was only getting unemployment pay of £2.50 a week and made up for it with my own cash that was sent in by family and friends. Had I gone to work in the machine shop sewing towels I would have earned £7 a week, but I refused on principle to get a job. I had always been a hard worker but after being falsely accused of something and then being sent to one of the country's biggest hovels for further assessment, I drew the line. I was only punishing myself but when I set my mind to something, I stick to it.

Letters from my family and Christine helped me cope as I had little freedom here; only let out of my cell to collect meals and for two hours' association on an evening and a bit more at weekends. I don't think I have had worse food (if you could call it food) in all the years of being incarcerated. The salads were swarming with black fly, greenfly and little slugs, and everything else was oily or greasy. I don't expect a fine-dining menu, but no one deserves to eat this filth. I was told they'd recently had a £3 million kitchen installed. It is anyone's guess what they produced before that. A new vandal-proof roof had also been installed at a cost of around £33 million. That was a hoot as apart from a handful of Category D inmates, everyone was escorted everywhere.

Winter was fast approaching and it was cold. Out on the landings it was so hot that you went around in T-shirts, but back in the cell it was another matter and you'd wear every item of clothing you could find. I had to don two pairs of socks to wear as gloves, which made writing very difficult. This was hindering my progress because I was trying to make sense of the material I'd received from the solicitors and raise awareness of my case. I had to take the gloves off to write but I could only complete about three lines before I had to put them on again. My finger joints were freezing and could barely move. I was not permitted to have my battery-powered typewriter and had to make do with a manual model instead. At least it allowed me to get my correspondence to lawyers presentable, as well as my parole application.

The inside of the cell's back wall was a sheet of ice, at least a quarter of an inch thick, and that was with the heating on. The heating pipes were barely warm. Winston would put a mat on his bed at night to preserve the heat, but as I was only looking to be there in the short term, I didn't have one. They could only be handed in on visits but I didn't get any visitors. Hot water for drinks would be totally cold within about five minutes and as I was denied my china mug, I had a prison-issue plastic cup in which drinks tasted awful. It was so cold, you could see your breath form into little white clouds. I don't know how any of us survived the cold and if anyone complained, staff would turn the heating off for three days.

Christmas was just like any other day, with the exception of some processed turkey, stuffing and Christmas pudding. The only extra we got was association during lunchtime, when we were normally locked up, but we were still locked up at 4.00 pm as usual. On Boxing Day and New Year's Day, nothing changed from the normal routine. We still woke in a freezing cell to dress as quickly as possible in clothes that were damp from the cold. As with all Victorian prisons, the windows were high up and the only way to see out was to stand on the bed, and even then you might only be able to see a hint of skyline or a bit of some buildings. It wasn't exactly a room with a view. In Victorian times, the high windows allowed more light into the cell before electricity was introduced. While the cells had been altered and modernized (a little), they retained many of their archaic features, which meant they were not really fit for purpose. So the recesses, which once held a candle to allow light in from behind a thick piece of glass, were now bricked up. The walls also bore evidence of past times, in the form of carvings and graffiti. Still, the overall regime at Dartmoor was more lenient than in the Victorian era. Winston showed me the pictures he was using to illustrate his book and it brought home to me just how grim it was in those days.

A hot shower was a small pleasure. However, it was a case of first come first served before the water started to run warm, then tepid. Everyone would try and get the end corner shower as it wasn't visible from the landing, otherwise you'd be gawped at by the female staff who obviously got some kind of thrill from their voyeurism. Most of the staff on my wing were frosty towards inmates. It may have been because as well as housing anyone waiting for an assessment, it was also home to the sex offenders. I never got to transfer to another wing, so I can't make a comparison. Some inmates were moved on to the wing for the purpose of assessment and then moved back, while others, like me, who had gone there from reception would only be allocated a wing following assessment. It was difficult to integrate because while you were on this wing, inmates assumed you were a sex offender and sex offenders got a hard time in prison. Some inmates would have to be placed in isolation for their own protection, which is known as Rule 43. There is also Rule 43B, which is when an inmate is placed in isolation to protect other inmates. Those on 43B are usually relocated to another prison and may end up being transferred several times until they settle down, which they usually do after a period of total isolation.

Chapter 11

HMP Littlehey
January 1997-February 2001
The Beginning of the End

HMP Littlehey is a Category C male prison, primarily, but not exclusively, for sex offenders. It is situated in the village of Perry near Huntingdon in Cambridgeshire and although the site had once been home to Gaynes Hall Youth Custody Centre, it was demolished and rebuilt as Littlehey in 1988, nine years before I arrived in January 1997.

Like The Verne, Littlehey also ran the Listener scheme and despite the problems I'd had before, I wanted to give it another go. I contacted

Unknown man pictured in Littlehey Prison.

the Samaritans who told me my previous situation would not go against me, so I applied and was one of around forty to get through to interview. After passing that, I was among the twenty-five selected to undergo training, which was two hours on a Saturday morning for sixteen weeks. While The Verne had been the first prison to run the scheme, Littlehey was one of the last and by this time, the training had improved. Over the sixteen weeks, about a quarter dropped out and another quarter failed. That left twelve fully trained Listeners, of which I was one. After the training, a fellow inmate, Richard, was appointed co-ordinator for the group and it was a role he did very well. We became good friends knowing that we could rely on each other for support and that we could discuss any problems without it going to the group. Every association period we would meet up and walk round the grounds, watch TV or play cards. Richard was serving seven years for being the getaway driver on an armed robbery – something he never wanted a part of but was talked into by his brother. It was the first and only time he was in trouble with the law. While bad news for him, his incarceration was good fortune on my part as Richard, who had about two years left to serve, was like the brother I never had. He became friendly with my family and, as he didn't get many visitors, he even sent them a visiting order (a prisoner's request for a visit) and they came and visited us both.

About a year into our roles, I was told during lunchtime lock-up that I was the new Listener co-ordinator as Richard was being 'ghosted' out. I was speechless and when I did find my voice I just asked, 'Why?' and 'Where to?' The PO in charge of the Listener scheme said it was a security matter and he couldn't tell me there and then but would meet me after unlock. When the time came, I shot round to his office as fast as I could and he made us both a cup of coffee. He told me that if I wanted the Listener co-ordinator job, he would inform the workshop – where I had been production manager on electronics, making talking appliances for the blind and control panels for supermarket freezers – that I would not be working there any more. I told him I did. It was a full-time position and would mean a drop in wages from £18 to £12 a week but it didn't matter as I wanted to see the job done properly, even though I didn't know all that it entailed and I wouldn't be able to see Richard to find out. It transpired that he had been having an affair with one of the visiting female Samaritans! She was no longer allowed to visit any prison in a professional capacity, so she resigned from the Samaritans and visited him in the same way any other person would. Richard, meanwhile, was transferred to HMP Wellingborough.

I was surprised that he hadn't told me about the affair and, in a letter, I asked him why. He said it wasn't that he didn't trust me, he was concerned that if they were caught – as they were – and if the authorities thought I knew about it, it could affect my chances of progressing through the system. As punishment, three months were added on to his sentence. We kept in touch and exchanged letters on a weekly basis at the same time as I was co-ordinating the Listener scheme, which I ran with a rod of iron, removing people if I felt they weren't fit for the job. Following Richard's release, he came to visit me three or four times and he kept me informed of his news. He was back working and was still seeing Sue, the ex-Samaritan. Then it was my turn to tell him my news – I'd got bail pending my appeal hearing.

Before my release, Richard told me that he and Sue were getting married and asked me to be his best man. I was truly honoured. I asked about his brothers but he said he had little to do with his family, and it was his brothers who had got him into trouble with the law. He told me I would need a passport as it was going to be on a beach in Jamaica, and my family were invited all expenses paid. I was thrilled. But about a month later, Sue called to say Richard was in hospital. He'd had a post-work drink in in a pub, played a fruit machine and won £120. When he left to go home, he was followed by three youths and mugged. His injuries were so severe that he never regained consciousness and he died. The youths were arrested but were laughing and sniggering in court and were given just six months in prison. My family and I attended Richard's funeral and went back to his family's house for the wake. Unfortunately, I was never in touch with them again and within about six months Sue stopped answering my calls and replying to my letters.

In the summer of 1997, Don Hale was examining the possible links of two other unsolved murders to that of Wendy Sewell's. Both had occurred during 1970 and similarities had been made by Cheshire and Derbyshire forces who were investigating them. The first case concerned 18-year-old Jacqueline 'Jackie' or 'Jacci' Ansell-Lamb who was found face down and half-naked in Square Wood, Mere, near Knutsford, Cheshire on 14 March 1970, some six days after she was last seen hitchhiking at the start of the M1 in London. She had been trying to get home to Manchester. Her blue and white miniskirt was beside her and her body was wrapped in her purple-coloured coat. She had been raped and strangled. The second case was that of student teacher Barbara Mayo. On Monday, 12 October 1970, 24-year-old Barbara left her London address around 8.00 am in order to hitch-hike to Catterick, North Yorkshire. Six days later her body was found, with her clothing in disarray and with her jacket spread over her, in a wood near Ault Hucknall in Derbyshire. She had also been raped and strangled. In December 1996, the then Chief Constable of West Yorkshire Police, Keith Hellawell, appeared in a television documentary entitled *Silent Victims*, which referred to the Ansell-Lamb and Mayo cases. Hellawell believed they had both been committed by the Yorkshire Ripper, Peter Sutcliffe. Some eighteen years later, former police intelligence officer Chris Clark would reach the same conclusion while researching attacks and murders he believed to bear the Ripper's hallmarks. The crimes remain unsolved.

Don noted the similarities between those cases and Wendy Sewell's. Although there was no mention of Wendy being strangled in the post-mortem report written by pathologist Alan Usher, Don's medium, Christine Smith, raised the matter of strangulation when she felt a tightening around her throat after visiting the scene of Wendy's attack in Bakewell Cemetery. Furthermore, Don had seen mortuary photographs and stated that there did appear to be bruising around her neck. He submitted a report to Derbyshire Police and just a few weeks later the force organized a press conference to announce that they were re-opening the Barbara Mayo case after twenty-seven years. Their first press release stated that they were to 'disclose a major new development in their hunt for the person responsible.' A few days later, another press release was released which said:

> 'A scientific breakthrough has meant that a DNA sample has been obtained from clothing worn by the victim at the scene. At a press conference today the man leading the investigation Assistant Chief Constable Don Dovaston said: "The police never forget and our files in relation to this matter have not closed. During twenty-seven years someone must have shown signs that others will have picked up on. I am appealing to these people to come forward and speak to us."'

On New Year's Day 1998, I penned a letter to Don:

> 'Dear Don, Can I wish you and your family a very happy
> New Year. As from this Saturday I will be able to function
> as a Listener affiliated to the Samaritans. [My solicitor]
> John Atkins is pleased that I have been selected for training
> and sees it as a good thing as it can be put forward at my
> next parole review if I do not get my appeal. As you rightly
> say this year looks like it could be an interesting one all
> round. I was pleased to read that John Atkins and [ITV news
> reporter] Paul Taylor should have their legal submissions
> ready for the CCRC [Criminal Cases Review Commission]
> by the third week of this month. I hope that it will be met
> with very little opposition. Thank you again for all that you
> have done for me. Perhaps this year you will see your efforts
> rewarded. Yours sincerely, Stephen.'

By the middle of 1999, progress with the CCRC seemed to grind to
a halt. This was extremely frustrating and resulted in my MP, Patrick
McLoughlin, raising the matter in the House of Commons. He asked
the Leader of the House Margaret Beckett if the Home Secretary could
make a statement on the progress. Mrs Beckett replied:

> 'The honourable gentleman will know that we inherited
> long delays in many parts of the criminal justice system.
> That is a source of concern to the Government, as it rightly
> is to the public and we are trying to take steps to diminish
> those delays. That applies too, to the Criminal Cases Review
> Commission. Ministers are aware of and are concerned
> about the delays and we are considering what can be done
> to ease the position.'

The delays continued throughout 1999 and well into 2000. That year
I was awarded £500 in an out-of-court settlement at the European
Court of Human Rights after complaining that I had not been given the
opportunity to contest my continued incarceration. On 14 November
2000 I was at Littlehey Prison, packed and ready as usual in case I was
going to be released straight away, when just before 3.00 pm, Patrick

McLoughlin telephoned Don to see if a decision by the CCRC had been made. Shortly afterwards a fax message reached Don's office:

'The Criminal Cases Review Commission has referred the conviction of Mr Stephen Leslie Downing to the Court of Appeal. Mr Downing was convicted on 15 February 1974 at Nottingham Crown Court of the murder of Mrs Wendy Sewell. He was sentenced to be detained at Her Majesty's Pleasure. His appeal against conviction was dismissed by the Court of Appeal on 25 October 1974. Mr Downing applied to the Home Office for a review of his conviction. His application was transferred to the Criminal Cases Review Commission for consideration on 31 March 1997 when it assumed responsibility for the review of suspected miscarriage of justice.'

I was elated! But my joy was tempered by the realization that, whatever happened, I would have to remain a prisoner for some time. Eventually, Derbyshire Police issued the following press statement: 'The Derbyshire Constabulary has cooperated with the CCRC during their inquiry. This cooperation will continue during the appeal hearing.' A police spokesman said the force would have to reconsider opening the murder case if the appeal found I was not responsible for Wendy Sewell's murder. He added: 'We can't discuss evidence in public, although others can. It's all subject to the appeal.'

On 8 December 2000, I wrote to Don:

'Dear Don, This is just a personal note of thanks for all the support you have given me and my family over the last twelve months and at times when you have put aside your own problems. I don't know who would have devoted so much time to a campaign as you have and I should like to extend my note of gratitude to your long-suffering family for their understanding. I hope that we have at last come to the end of what has seemed a never-ending journey. I would like you and your family to enjoy the best Christmas you have ever had and I hope the coming New Year holds lots of joys and happiness. With warmest best wishes Stephen Downing.'

Finally, a date was set for a bail hearing. It would be in the High Court in London on 15 December 2000 and would result in my first family Christmas at home for twenty-eight years. But it was not to be. The Crown Prosecutor Julian Bevan had only had the case paperwork for ten days, had not had time to read it and was ill-prepared, and furthermore, was off on an extended holiday. The presiding judge gave Mr Bevan another month to study the file and refused the application for bail, so I had to suffer a further enforced stay in Littlehey. It was shattering. When Don called I said: 'My family and I are used to setbacks, but it is heartbreaking. I'll be thinking of them at Christmas and I'm sure they'll be thinking of me.'

This extract is from *The Guardian*, Saturday, 16 December 2000:

'Freedom delayed after 27 years – the lawyers aren't ready. Stephen Downing, who supporters claim is the victim of Britain's longest-running miscarriage of justice, learned yesterday he would spend his 28th Christmas in prison because of a legal bungle at the court of appeal.

'Supporters of Mr Downing, who was jailed in 1974 for the murder of Wendy Sewell, a typist, reacted with fury when he was denied bail after a barrister for the crown prosecution service confessed he had not had time to prepare his side of the case which had been referred back to the appeal court.

'Julian Bevan QC, who left Britain last night for a Christmas trip to Africa, said he had only been notified of yesterday's high court bail hearing at 4.30pm the day before. "I received briefing papers 10 days ago. I was not aware that a bail application would be made and therefore I did not read the papers with any degree of urgency," he told the court. "I am not in a position to give the merits or demerits of the crown position because this takes considerable analysis."

'However, Mr Bevan, referring to prison psychiatric reports which say that Downing is "in denial" of murder, urged that the court should be "slow in granting bail".

'The judge, Mr Justice Crane, said that without a view from the prosecution bail could only be granted when the prospects of success at appeal were clear:

'"This is not one of those clear cases or straightforward cases in which it is right to grant bail." Downing, 44, had his case referred back to the appeal court by the criminal cases review commission on November 14. The bail hearing was told that an investigation by the CCRC had cast doubt on the reliability of the confession Downing made on the day of the murder, and on the forensic evidence.

'Don Hale, editor of the *Matlock Mercury*, who has campaigned for the former cemetery gardener's release for six years, said the prisoner and his parents would be devastated: "I think we're all stunned by the decision. It is another ridiculous statement. The crown prosecution service has had 27 years to prepare for this case. The CCRC has had it for three and a half years. Stephen Downing is in jail for his 28th Christmas for a crime he didn't commit." Downing's father Ray, 66, a taxi driver who still lives in Bakewell where the murder was committed in 1973, said the family were resigned to the court's decision. Patrick McLoughlin, Downing's MP, described the circumstances surrounding the bail hearing as outrageous and demanded a statement from a minister in the Commons yesterday.

'A spokesman for the CPS blamed the defence for not serving notice of the bail hearing until Wednesday. Downing, who was 17 at the time, but had the reading age of an 11-year-old, was taken into custody by Derbyshire constabulary after he found Ms Sewell badly battered but still alive in the graveyard where he worked.

'His counsel, Edward Fitzgerald QC, yesterday outlined at the bail hearing the main findings of the CCRC. Downing's confession and the forensic evidence, "the two main planks" of the original prosecution case, had been undermined. He had been denied a lawyer during his police interview despite repeated requests, the court heard. At the original trial, a forensic examination of his bloodstained jeans had helped convict him, but an expert who looked again at the evidence expressed "serious concerns," Mr Fitzgerald said. Downing can renew his appeal for bail if the prosecution takes a favourable view after studying the case. It has been given until January 20 to do so.'

The new bail hearing was announced for Wednesday, 7 February 2001. Despite all my knockbacks over the years, I truly believed that, on that day, something was about to happen for the Crown QC Julian Bevan confirmed that the application for bail would not be contested. Although acting for the Crown he was heavily critical of Derbyshire Police and their actions from 1973. He said:

> 'I am happy to accept in this case there is a very real possibility that the rights he was entitled to were never brought to his attention. All the indications are they were not. Applying present-day standards the Crown recognizes that a failure to inform a prisoner in custody of his rights would be regarded as a serious breach, as of course, would a failure to caution a suspect at the appropriate moment.'

The Crown was not opposing bail, which meant that I had to be released immediately. The Judge Mr Justice Pitchford confirmed that I was being released on bail pending appeal and I was free to go.

That afternoon as I walked out of Littlehey and custody for the first time since 13 September 1973, more than twenty-seven years earlier. I had been taken in as a 17-year-old youth and here I was a 44-year-old man nearing middle-age. So many things had changed in the outside world. When the great doors slid open, I stepped out alone, quietly dignified in my navy blue suit and purple tie, and was met by the warm sun and a blast of television camera lights.

Chapter 12

I Walk Free After Twenty-Seven Years

The Daily Telegraph, 7 February 2001:

> 'Stephen Downing the man jailed 27 years ago for a murder he claims he did not commit walked free from jail today after being granted bail by the Court of Appeal. Grinning broadly and dressed in a dark blue suit with purple tie, he emerged into the sunlight from Littlehey jail in Cambridgeshire at 4.12pm. He shook hands with a prison officer and then left with two reporters from a Sunday newspaper. He said: "I would like to thank all the public and the media for their support and help. I am elated and I now hope to spend some

Delighted with my first taste of freedom, outside Littlehey Prison.

valuable time with my family." Downing, 44, was released to await the hearing of an appeal against his conviction and life jail sentence for the killing of the married typist Wendy Sewell. Her badly-beaten body was found in a cemetery where he worked in his home town of Bakewell, Derbyshire.

'Bail was not opposed by the Crown, which conceded that the appeal was highly likely to succeed in the light of serious questions raised over the admissibility of Downing's confession statements which formed a main plank of the prosecution case. Downing was 17 at the time of the killing but had the mental age of an 11-year-old. He has consistently denied murder and so has been ineligible for parole, which could have given him freedom 10 years ago. The Criminal Cases Review Commission referred his case to the Court of Appeal after years of campaigning by his parents, Ray and Juanita, and by Don Hale, editor of the local newspaper the *Matlock Mercury*. Bail was granted by Mr Justice Pitchford after a 40-minute hearing in London. The judge said that, having read the case papers, he agreed with Crown lawyers that the conviction would probably be quashed on appeal – although the court may ultimately take a different view. Conditions of Downing's bail were not disclosed in court, but Mr Hale said afterwards that he must live at home with his parents and report to his local police station. Mr Hale said Downing's parents had also put up a £5,000 surety.

'His counsel Edward Fitzgerald, QC said Downing, who had reported finding the body, was taken to the police station at 2.30 pm and interrogated for more than seven hours, on and off before being cautioned at 10.30 pm. It was then that he made oral and written confessions. During all that he was never told by police that he was under arrest or in custody and was not told of his rights of access to a solicitor. There was strong reason to believe that he did ask for a lawyer but his request was denied. In the light of these breaches of the Judges' Rules on interrogation of suspects, the confession statements should have been ruled inadmissible.

'Mr Fitzgerald said: "There is a most powerful case for saying that this conviction is unsafe. For this man, who has served 27 years, to serve a day longer would not be just." In court, Julian Bevan, QC, for the Crown, said the police had good grounds for suspecting Downing – blood on his trousers and the fact that he had used the murder weapon, a pickaxe handle, in his work. But the Crown had to accept that there was a very real possibility that the rights he was entitled to were never brought to his attention. And he should have been cautioned much earlier. By present day standards, those were serious breaches of the rules. Oddly, the admissibility of the confessions was not raised by defence lawyers at the trial, or in an earlier unsuccessful appeal in 1974, or at any time since – until the case reached the Review Commission. "This point has lain dormant for over 25 years and has been sitting there, obvious to any criminal lawyer, and has been completely missed," he said. Mr Bevan said recent investigations, including those conducted by the Review Commission, did not support the assertion by the newspaper editor and others that there was evidence of another person being responsible for the murder. But in the light of the question mark over the confessions and the possibility that they would have been ruled inadmissible had they been challenged at trial "the Crown cannot properly submit that the verdict of the jury would have been the same."

'Downing's parents later left their Bakewell home clutching a card with the message "To Steve xxx" written on the envelope. Before being driven away, Mr Downing said: "We would like to say we are delighted, nothing else, just delighted." A spokesman earlier read a brief statement on their behalf: "The Downings are absolutely over the moon and delighted with the news. It has not sunk in yet and they are both rather emotional. They don't know what their plans are and don't know if he is coming straight back." But the victim's husband, David Sewell, said he remained convinced that Downing was guilty. Mr Sewell, who still lives in the house in Middleton-by-Youlgreave near Bakewell which he shared with his late wife, was at today's court hearing. He said: "You know the evidence as well I do. It was presented and he was found guilty and nothing has come to light since that would cast doubt on that. It might if you read the newspapers, but it certainly doesn't if you listened in court. If I see him in Bakewell I won't cross the street but I won't stop to talk to him either." Mr Sewell's second wife Jennifer, whom he wed in 1984, said: "I thought it might turn out this way but we will be getting on with life as usual. We go into Bakewell a lot and if we pass him in the street, so be it."'

Life as a free man was strange. I had, after all, spent my entire adult life in prison. At first I would cross the road to avoid meeting people as I wasn't sure how they'd react. As time moved on, I began to realize a lot of people were on my side and supported me and my fight for justice to clear my name.

On Tuesday, 15 January 2002, I went with my parents and sister to the Court of Appeal in the Strand for my CCRC appeal. It was reported that at least 100 reporters, photographers and camera crews from media organizations worldwide were waiting to greet me, my family, Don Hale and his wife Kath. The atmosphere was electric and we were full of excitement and optimism. My appeal was due to start at 10.30 am but before we could enter the court, we had to do a number of interviews. There was an overwhelming buzz from the Fleet Street pack who were quite obviously 100 per cent behind my cause.

The entrance doors to court number 6 opened just before 10.00 am and people scrambled to get the best seats. Just before 10.30 am, I entered the dock escorted by a female warder and acknowledged my family who were sitting opposite. Almost immediately the three Law Lords – Lord Justice Pill, Mrs Justice Hallett and Mr Justice Davis – entered from a door behind the bench and we rose. The hearing was as follows:

'R. v. Stephen Downing [2002] EWCA Crim 263'
'15 January 2002 – Court of Appeal (Criminal Division)
In February 1974 Downing, then 17 years old and of good character, was convicted of murder. He was sentenced to be detained during Her Majesty's pleasure. In October 1974

application for leave to appeal against conviction and for leave to call a witness was made. The only ground for the application for leave to appeal was that a 16 year old girl [Jayne Atkins was 15] had, after the trial, made a statement in which she claimed to have seen the victim alive at a time shortly after Downing was alleged to have murdered her. The court heard evidence from the girl, but concluded that it was not credible and refused the application for leave to appeal against conviction.

'The deceased Wendy Sewell, was an office worker with the Forestry Commission in Derbyshire. She received numerous blows to the head when present in a cemetery during her lunch break in September 1973. She sustained fractures to the skull. There was evidence that there must have been at least seven or eight violent blows with an implement such as a pickaxe helve or handle.

'Downing worked for the local authority in the cemetery and lived nearby. It was he who, at about 1.20pm, reported to the cemetery attendant, Mr Walker, that a woman had been attacked in the cemetery. To Mr Walker Downing seemed very calm. The two men went into the cemetery and saw Sewell. Other employees, and later the police, arrived at the scene. Sewell was naked up to the thighs with blood on her face, hair, hands and lower stomach. Her top clothing had been pulled above her breasts. There was evidence that after help arrived she tried to wipe blood from her eyes with the back of her hand and tried unsuccessfully to stand up. A splintered and blood stained pickaxe helve was found nearby.

'On her way to hospital in an ambulance Sewell was still alive, very restless and throwing her right arm out wildly. She tried to push away people who were attempting to care for her. She died in hospital two days later as a result of the injuries sustained in the cemetery. When he was observed by Mr Walker and the others Downing's clothing was blood stained, especially his trousers and his boots.

'The prosecution case depended first, of course, on the presence of Downing near the scene at about the material time and the fact that the pickaxe helve was normally stored in the unconsecrated chapel at the cemetery used as a store house and to which Downing had access in the course of his work.

'The evidence consisted of the oral and written admissions which Downing made later on 12 September. Reliance was placed upon scientific evidence about the blood staining of his clothes which was claimed to show a close relationship between Downing's trousers and boots and the injuries inflicted by the pickaxe helve. The contact with Mrs Sewell which Downing admitted would not explain all the blood staining on Downing's trousers and boots.

'The prosecution called a forensic scientist, Mr Lee. In his written report Mr Lee had said that the blood staining on Downing's clothing "might well be described as a textbook example of the pattern of blood staining which might be expected on the clothing of the assailant in a wounding such as that which Wendy Sewell suffered." The court has admitted further scientific evidence. Reports have been obtained from Mr Stockdale on behalf of Downing and from Mr Wain, an independent forensic scientist instructed by the CCRC. At trial a defence scientist, Mr Moss, was present, but, for reasons which are not obvious, was not called. His evidence was certainly a good deal less favourable to the prosecution than was that of Mr Lee.

'Both scientists who have now reported are critical of the opinions of Mr Lee as expressed in his report and in his oral evidence. Some of the criticisms are made on the basis of developments in the science since 1973. The result is that Mr Stockdale states in his report that the blood staining is equally consistent with Downing's account in evidence that he had contact with the deceased only after she had been seriously injured, as it was with his guilt of the offence.

'The prosecution have not sought leave to cross-examine Mr Stockdale. Mr Wain in his report stated that the blood staining did give some support for the prosecution case, but described that support as weak. Mr Wain's opinion now is the same as that of Mr Stockdale, that the scientific evidence is as consistent with innocence as with guilt.

'It is clear that the evidence of blood staining cannot now be relied on in support of a submission that the conviction was safe. We have referred to those who saw Mrs Sewell in the cemetery. There was evidence that Downing made a number of comments, some of which, arguably, supported the case against him. Mr Walker stated that Downing said, "I don't want to lose my job. I like it." Mr Dawson, one of the council employees present, said that there was nothing unusual about Downing when the seriously injured woman was found. Mr Fox, another council employee, said that while they were present the woman moved, whereupon Downing said, "There looks like being an identification parade." He also was alleged by witnesses to have said, "It was not me, honest. I only found her. She was down there," and "I have been using that pickaxe today but it was not me." Downing later denied making most of the arguably damaging statements.

'PC Ball was the first police officer on the scene. He tried first aid on Mrs Sewell, who resisted violently with her arm. Downing said, "It isn't me, honest, it isn't. Don't blame me, I have not done it." He was plainly blood stained. He said, "Look, these came when I turned her over." Downing later said that he had not used the pickaxe handle on that day. Constable Ball thought that Downing was in an excited state. The officer in charge of the investigation, Divisional DI Younger, attended the scene at 2.30 pm. He questioned Downing who was then taken to the police station. Before the jury was evidence of what happened at the police station and of some of the interviews which took place. Downing was not cautioned. He did not have the benefit of legal advice. Eventually he was cautioned late in the evening. Having been cautioned at 10.45 pm, he admitted to Constable Charlesworth: "I did do it but I don't know what made me do it." DI Younger then was called back into the room. Downing repeated his admission. He then made a written statement, having been reminded of his caution. We will refer to the events at the police station in more detail. In his evidence Downing denied the offence. He denied some of the statements to witnesses. He described the interviews which he underwent. He said that he was treated with consideration and provided with tea. He said he had done it when it was not true because he was tired, hungry, and his back hurt. He was only just able to keep awake. DI Younger put his hand on Downing's shoulder twice to shake him. He had had trouble with his back for two years after a fall at school. He signed the statement but it was untrue. He made it because he believed the police would question him all night if necessary and he did not realise that the woman was badly hurt.

'He also said that when he first found the seriously injured woman he had touched between her breasts to see if her heart was beating and he put his hands between her legs and put his finger up her vagina. [I did not touch her between the legs: it has been proven forensically that she was not sexually assaulted]. She started to move. She raised herself up into a sitting position, shook her head violently and put her hands behind her head. We add in passing that one of the reasons for the scientists considering that the blood staining is not evidence of guilt is that no sufficient, or any, consideration was given to the possibility that it was in the course of her movements of her shaking her head and of her exhalation in the presence of Downing that the blood may have reached his clothing.

'Since 1974 considerable efforts have been made by Downing's father, Mr Ray Downing, and by Mr Don Hale, former editor of the *Matlock Mercury*, to have the case reopened. Acknowledgment is made of the help given by Ray Downing and Don Hale. The issue now in the forefront of Downing's case, the admissibility and reliability of the confessions, has been explored and analysed fully only since the case was referred to the CCRC in 1997. Their admissibility was not challenged at the trial. In his summing-up the judge referred to certain questions, put on behalf of Downing, to which we will refer in a moment. The judge noted, however, that counsel on behalf of the defence: "made the comment in so many words, I allege no impropriety on the part of the police." Downing was represented at the trial by leading counsel of great experience, Mr Dennis Barker QC, and by junior counsel Mr Warren, now Mr Warren QC. No point on the admissibility of the confessions was raised on the application for permission to appeal to this court in 1974. Mr Dennis Barker had given an opinion about appeal, in the course of which he stated: "The Crown's case rested in large measure on oral admissions and a written statement made by the accused to the police. No objection could have been or was made to the admissibility of this evidence. Mr Downing could not, and did not, give any real reason why he made such admissions.

'Giving the judgment of this court in 1974, Orr LJ confirmed: "No suggestion was made that there had been any improper behaviour on the part of the police." Mr Fitzgerald QC, on behalf of Downing, has helpfully taken the court, carefully and in some detail, through the events at the police station on 12 September. He submits that Downing should have been cautioned as soon as 3.15pm on 12 September. He submits that in the absence of a caution at the appropriate time and having regard to the extreme youth of Downing and the fact that he is only of low average intelligence, together with the fact that he was not told of his right to obtain legal advice, together with the fact that he was in effect kept in custody for approaching eight hours before the confession was made, it should not have been admitted at the trial. Moreover whether it was admitted or not there is a serious question as to the reliability of the confessions made.

'It is noteworthy that there is no continuous account of what happened during the time between 2.30 and 10.30pm. The statement of Constable Charlesworth begins with an interview only in the evening. There is a statement from Det Sgt Wilson, but only of a brief conversation which took place, he says, at 7.10pm. There is a reference to a short interview with DI Younger between 3.15pm and 3.30pm. The practice at that time was not to keep the continuous record which is now required.

'The CCRC obtained statements from the two senior officers involved in the investigation, DI Younger and DCI Johnson. Unfortunately, Constable Charlesworth is dead. Mr Younger states that his recollection is that Constable Charlesworth was with Mr Downing most, if not all, of the time. Mr Johnson states: "I am quite sure that when he was taken from the cemetery to the police station his status was that of a witness assisting with police enquiries. Clearly at some stage his status changed and I cannot say when. I believe it is fair to say that from a very early point Stephen Downing was suspected of attacking the woman." Dealing with the basis on which Downing was present at the police station, Mr Johnson states: "The answer to that is that had he wanted to leave the police station he would not been allowed to do so. Looking back now, my belief is that he was under arrest whilst at the police station. Had Stephen Downing been arrested, I would have expected him to have been informed of his rights which would have included access to legal advice."

'We have been referred to the Judges' Rules which were in operation at the material time. They are now replaced by procedures laid down under the Police and Criminal Evidence Act 1984: "Every person at any stage of an investigation should be able to communicate and to consult privately with a solicitor. This is so even if he is in custody provided that in such a case no unreasonable delay or hindrance is caused to the processes of investigation or the administration of justice by his doing so." It cannot be suggested that any such hindrance was present in this case. In relation to statements from people interviewed, it is provided: "It is a fundamental condition of the admissibility in evidence against any person, equally of any oral answer given by that person to a question put by a police officer that of any statement made by that person, that it shall have been voluntary, in the sense that it has not been obtained from him by fear of prejudice or hope of advantage, exercised or held out by a person in authority, or by oppression."

'The principle is overriding and applicable in all cases. Within that principle the following rules are put forward as a guide to police officers conducting investigations. Nonconformity with these rules may render answers and statements liable to be excluded from evidence in subsequent criminal proceedings. Rule II provides: "As soon as a police officer has evidence which would afford reasonable grounds for suspecting that a person has committed an offence, he shall caution that person or cause him to be cautioned before putting to him any questions, or further questions, relating to that offence." The caution shall be in the following terms: "You are not obliged to say anything unless you wish to do so but what you say may be put into writing and given in evidence." It is submitted that there has been no relevant alteration in the procedures to be followed. That point is relevant because it is common ground that the court should, when assessing the fairness of events before 1984, have regard to the now applicable procedures for ensuring the fairness of treatment of suspects in police stations. However, it is said we should now have regard to the subsection which provides: "If in any proceedings where the prosecution proposes to give in evidence a confession made [by] an accused person, it is represented to the court that the confession was or may been obtained (a) by oppression of the person who made it; or (b) in consequence of anything said or done which was likely, in the circumstances existing at the time, to render unreliable any confession which might be made by him in consequence thereof, the court shall not allow the confession to be given in evidence against him except insofar as the prosecution prove to the court beyond reasonable doubt that the confession, notwithstanding that it may be true, was not obtained as aforesaid."

'Counsel concur in the view that the concept of "oppression" is thereby extended to cover a more general consideration of the circumstances in which a confession was made. It is submitted that what the officers did before 10.30pm on 12 September amounted to interrogation and not mere enquiries. It cannot be suggested that this 17 year old was offered legal assistance, or told of his right to obtain it. That, in our judgment, is a serious breach of the treatment which should have been afforded to him. The Crown accepts that there were substantial and significant breaches of the Judges' Rules on the afternoon and evening of 12 September. It does not accept the 3.15pm time for the cautioning but submits that by 7.10pm there was a strong case for cautioning, and by 8.45pm that case was overwhelming. In selecting those times counsel has regard to the presence by then of conflicting statements by Downing and to the scientific witness's then provisional view that the blood staining was not consistent with the limited contact with the injured woman which Downing accepted. The record of interviews placed before the court was sparse. Counsel has underlined the isolation to which Downing was subjected. He had no friends or family and was not told of his right to legal advice. We regard such isolation of a 17 year old as being a very significant factor in this case.

'No criticism has been or is made of the summing-up of the judge or of the judge's conduct of the trial. The judge was entitled to have regard, when considering the way the defence case was being put, to the great experience and expertise of leading counsel appearing for Downing. The admissibility of the confession was not challenged. The judge referred to the confessions and to Downing's denial of them. He stated: "It was put, you remember, that as the hours wore by this young man became tired, and you may have little hesitation in concluding that if a suspect is falling asleep and having to be shaken it is no time to continue interrogation. That is bordering, you may think, on oppression if he is not given food and the rest of it. What was put, you see, to Mr Younger, there was this condition of tiredness and one officer had said, 'Admit it. We know you have done it' and another said, 'You will be questioned all night' and another one said he would bet his wages the accused would admit it before the night was out. Now, the reason that I present this problem to you in this way is that those questions would seem to indicate the suggestion of some measure of impropriety. Of course, there is the issue. The officers say firmly it is nonsense to talk about this young man not understanding what was going on or he was falling asleep, but this is the point, in spite of those questions, Mr Barker, on behalf of the defence, made the comment in so many words, "I allege no impropriety on the part of the police". And you must consider all that.

'There is no doubt that Downing's instructions were that the confessions had not been obtained voluntarily. We have been referred to the statements he gave to his solicitor before the trial. On 4 October he stated: "I was taken to the police station at 2.00pm, they started to question me and kept me until 11.00pm. I kept denying that I had done it. Eventually I got very tired and I started dropping to sleep. They said they would carry on all night with questions. Eventually I admitted to the attack. I did this because I was tired and wanted to get some sleep. Later, during the time I was being questioned, the police never threatened me but they did get hold of me by my shoulders and shake me because I wouldn't admit it. I asked if I could see my parents. At first they said no, but eventually my parents came. I asked my dad if I needed a solicitor but one of the policemen said I didn't. I had blood on the knees of my jeans and possibly on the soles of my feet. That got there whilst I was kneeling on the floor at the side of Wendy Sewell."

'Later [Downing stated]: "One of the policemen did say that he'd bet his wages I'd admit it before the night was out." There followed a statement of 22 November: "When Charlesworth started questioning me again after Younger had left I decided to admit to having attacked Wendy. I had asked at sometime between 9.00 and 10.00pm if I could see my parents and have a solicitor. Detective Inspector Younger would not let me have either."

'Those statements indicate that the instructions of Downing were of impropriety by the police in obtaining the confession from him. We find it extremely difficult to understand why the admissibility of the oral and written confessions was not challenged at the trial. We do bear in mind that the defence case was a difficult one to conduct. It was known that Downing's evidence was going to be that he had come across a half-naked and badly injured woman in the cemetery and, having touched her between the breasts to see if her heart was beating, he put his hands between her legs and put his finger up her vagina. That evidence was unlikely to commend him to a jury. We add that in a comparatively recent statement Downing has denied that that is what he said. However, it is clear from the judge's summing-up that he did use words to that effect. We find it inconceivable that counsel on such a significant matter would not have corrected the judge had he not accurately directed the jury as to the evidence which had been given.

'Defence counsel also knew that Downing had made admissions to doctors that he had struck Mrs Sewell with a pickaxe handle with a view to sexually assaulting her. Admissions were made to two doctors at the Risley Remand Centre [I did not admit this to any doctors at any point]. They were repeated to a consultant psychiatrist instructed by solicitors on Downing's behalf. We accept all those admissions are likely to have been made within about two weeks of 12 September. Subsequently it was denied that the admissions were true. It is possible that counsel took the view that in those circumstances allegations against police officers who were investigating the offence would be likely to lead to the jury taking an adverse view of Downing and his credibility. It is possible that counsel feared that his admissions to the doctors would be put to Downing in the course of his evidence. Counsel may have taken a tactical decision not to challenge the admissibility of the evidence, considering that Downing would be better served by an absence of allegations of impropriety and Downing's mere evidence that the confessions were untrue. We do find it very difficult to reconcile the assurance given to the judge that no impropriety was alleged with the few questions which were put.

'Downing has given an explanation for the withdrawal of the confessions. In a statement to his solicitor he referred to the visit he says that his father made to the police station: "When my father first saw me at the police station and asked if it was true that I had admitted to the attack I told him it was true. He said, 'Well, son, I am proud of you, not for doing it but for admitting it.' I kept that remark of my father's in my mind and this was one of the reasons why, for 13 days, I continued to tell him I was guilty. I felt pleased that my father was sticking by me and I did not know what he would say or how he would react if I were to tell him the truth. On 25 September 1973 I felt I just had to tell the truth and so I told him what really happened." There is some slight psychiatric support for the credibility of that explanation given. We are unable to understand leading counsel's reference in his advice on appeal to the fact that no explanation was given for the confessions being made.

'The issue of fact to which we have just referred is not for this court to resolve. It was an issue which could have been, but was not, raised at the trial. In our view, the trial was unsatisfactory by reason of the failure to challenge the admissibility of the confessions Downing made. His instructions were that the confessions were untrue and, what is more, had been obtained improperly. Questions alleging impropriety were put to police officers and yet counsel accepted that no impropriety on the part of the police was alleged.

'The test we should apply in circumstances such as these when considering whether the conviction is safe was stated in R v Ashley King (unreported) 10 December 1999: "We were invited by counsel at the outset to consider as a general question what the approach of the court should be in a situation such as this where a crime is investigated and a suspect interrogated and detained at a time when the statutory framework governing investigation, interrogation and detention was different from that now in force. We remind ourselves that our task is to consider whether this conviction is unsafe. If we do so consider it, the Criminal Appeal Act 1968 obliges us to allow the appeal. We should not (other things being equal) consider a conviction unsafe simply because of a failure to comply with a statute governing police detention, interrogation and investigation, which was not in force at the time. In looking at the safety of the conviction it is relevant to consider whether and to what extent a suspect may have been denied rights which he should have enjoyed under the rules in force at the time and whether and to what extent he may have lacked protections which it was later thought right that he should enjoy. But this court is concerned with the safety of the conviction. That is a question to be determined in the light of all the material before it, which will include the record of all the evidence in the case and not just an isolated part. If, in a case where the only evidence against a defendant was his oral confession which he had later retracted, it appeared that such confession was obtained in breach of the rules prevailing at the time and in circumstances which denied the defendant important safeguards later thought to be necessary to avoid the risk of a miscarriage of justice, there would be at least *prima facie* grounds for doubting the safety of the conviction. A very different thing from concluding that a defendant was necessarily innocent."

'Counsel are agreed that there were substantial and significant breaches of the Judges' Rules. Had the admissibility of the confession been challenged and impropriety by police officers alleged, it would have had a profound effect upon this trial. Confessions are excluded on the ground that they are not obtained voluntarily. Even if they are admitted, there remains the question whether they contain reliable admissions. In our judgment, had the matter been raised with the judge these confessions may well have been excluded by him. Even if they had been admitted, the jury would have been alerted to circumstances which may have rendered them unreliable. The Judges' Rules, and now the procedures under the Police and Criminal Evidence Act 1984, were promulgated to ensure fairness. In the absence of an investigation of the facts, with the Rules in mind, the jury may well, in a case such as the present, have been unaware of the real risks arising from the non-observance of

118

the Rules and the proper procedures. Had the matter been challenged, the jury's eyes would have been opened as to the risks.

'This court is aware of the unlikelihood, on the face of it, of someone sexually assaulting a badly injured woman, as Downing admits he did, unless it was he who had previously disabled her with sexual assault in mind. The court is also aware of the confessions made to several doctors in circumstances very different from those in the police station. The presence of Downing near the scene and the nature of the weapon must also be borne in mind. It is not, however, for this court to speculate as to what might have happened had the fundamental defect not been present. As Lord Bingham had recently underlined in R v Pendleton [2002]: "The question for its [the Court of Appeal's] consideration is whether the conviction is safe and not whether the accused is guilty." In the somewhat bizarre circumstances of this case we expressly do not address ourselves to the latter question.

'As to the confessions, if they are unreliable the conviction is unsafe. The safety of this conviction depends on the reliability of confessions made to the police on 12 September 1973. The court cannot be sure that the confessions were reliable. It follows that the conviction is unsafe. We do not speculate as to what might have happened if the defence had been conducted in a different way. For the reasons we have given this appeal is allowed and the conviction quashed.'

It was 3.50 pm. Five long hours after the hearing had begun, my life as a prisoner was over. I sat in the dock staring straight ahead at my family and waiting for the three judges to leave the room, not daring to show any emotion as the world's gaze was upon me. The second they left, I couldn't contain myself any longer. According to Don, my face lit up and I beamed as the court erupted. Family, friends, MPs, supporters, journalists and observers slapped each other on the back, hugged each other and even cried with relief. I was then led from the dock for one last time.

Don made his way out through the assembled crowd to a barrage of television lights, flashbulbs and questions and gave the following statement:

> 'I would have liked the judges to go a step further and say Stephen is innocent. They could have been more positive. I think Stephen will be a little disappointed. We want the case reopened – the real killer is still out there. I call upon the government to launch an enquiry into what went wrong all those years ago. I also think the Law Lords should have made some reference to the fact that Stephen has served ten years beyond his recommended tariff, simply because he continued to protest his innocence.'

I didn't mind Don appealing to the judges to say I was innocent as it echoed what my lawyers were saying. However, I did object to him pressing the police to admit that they were wrong when they said they weren't looking for anyone else in connection with the crime. My lawyers were working on that and I felt Don was stepping in where he was not wanted. He was also adamant that I should listen to him and ignore my lawyers' advice. He would not accept that they knew more about legalities than he did.

Nevertheless, today was for celebrating. The media wanted to see the star of the show so Don came and found me with my family talking to my legal team. We hugged and shook hands and slowly I walked out of court a free man with what Don described as the statesmanlike dignity that everyone had come to expect from me. I faced the assembled crowds and the world's press beaming from ear to ear and said:

> 'I hold no bitterness towards the Derbyshire police. They are now a different force altogether. It's all in the past. Let's forget it. I'd just like to say thank you to my family for all their support and care and also to my legal team and all my supporters.'

Chapter 13

A Second Life Sentence

I'd served twenty-seven years for a crime I didn't commit and had seen my sentence quashed by the highest court in the land. And yet my punishment did not end on that January morning. I was bombarded with insults and deliberately hurtful accusations from many parties, not least the British media. My private life – the first I'd ever had – was also raked over in public. To illustrate, here are extracts from articles and reports issued after my appeal, some of which would be written years after my release:

The Sunday Telegraph, 26 May 2002:

> 'Police are examining a tape recording in which Stephen Downing, whose conviction in the 1973 Bakewell graveyard murder was quashed by the Court of Appeal this year, allegedly confesses to the crime. Detectives, who reopened their investigation into the murder last month following intense media speculation that the "real" murderer was still at large, were handed the tape last Thursday. Officers examining the recording said last night that it "appeared to be genuine". The recording is apparently of conversations between Mr Downing, 46, and Christine Smith, his girlfriend, and was made following his release last year.
>
> 'A police spokesman said: "We have received a tape in relation to the reinvestigation of the 1973 murder of Wendy Sewell and are examining it." Although Mr Downing cannot be tried for the murder again, the appearance of fresh evidence may have an impact on his attempt to claim up to £1 million in compensation for his time spent in prison.
>
> 'Mrs Smith befriended Mr Downing while he was serving a life sentence for the murder of Mrs Sewell, who was bludgeoned and sexually assaulted while walking in the

Derbyshire town's cemetery in broad daylight… . He was released last year when it was revealed that detectives at the time had failed to caution him properly before he made his confession. Judges hearing Mr Downing's full appeal this year ruled the conviction to be unsafe but they were careful not to proclaim him innocent. His supporters and most of the media, however, greeted the verdict as proof that he was innocent.

'Don Hale, his chief supporter and a former local newspaper editor who has written a book espousing Mr Downing's innocence, claims that he was framed for the murder and that those really responsible have never been brought to justice.

'The BBC is preparing to film a dramatisation of Mr Hale's book. Mr Hale claims to have been the subject of a number of attempts on his life by the "real" murderers. Among them, he has claimed, was a lorry driver who tried to run him off the road. Police, however, say they have no record of Mr Hale reporting the events he describes. Mr Hale's book describes a web of Bakewell relationships involving locals who conspired to cover up the identity of the true killers while allowing Mr Downing to take the blame. He referred to Mrs Sewell as the "Bakewell Tart", alleging that she had been promiscuous and had been involved in a number of extramarital affairs.

'Mr Hale said last night: "Stephen's always been besotted with Christine Smith. She was a friend of the family and started visiting him in prison. I know their relationship has cooled in recent weeks and they have been having rows." Mrs Smith, who lives in Chesterfield and works as a medium, said: "I cannot say anything about what is in the tape. You will have to contact my solicitor." Chris Sellers, her lawyer, was unavailable for comment.'

The Guardian Saturday, 1 June 2002:

'I thought it was love. Now I know that I was wrong'

'Stephen Downing fell for the woman who backed his stand against wrongful conviction for murder. But now he feels betrayed and says she's a gold-digger, reports Amelia Hill.

'He is the victim of Britain's longest miscarriage of justice and she was his lifeline, maintaining her love for him and her belief in his innocence through his years in jail. But when the Court of Appeal quashed Stephen Downing's life sentence last year, a very different woman was waiting for him back in their Derbyshire home town: one who was not afraid to manipulate, deceive and, eventually, make secret recordings she said could send the man she claimed to love straight back to prison. Christine Smith, a 43-year-old, twice divorced grandmother, has spent the past eight years working her way into Downing's life, playing on the knowledge that Downing, imprisoned in 1973 for the murder of Wendy Sewell, had never had a girlfriend and was desperate to settle down. Although the relationship is now over, Smith has insisted her declarations of love were genuine. Downing himself, however, with his family and friends, is adamant the entire relationship was false and calculated. "Some people worried that she was more interested in a share of the millions of pounds Stephen is likely to receive in compensation payments," said Don Hale, former editor of the *Matlock Mercury* who spent eight years campaigning for Downing's release. "Christine kept Stephen on a string; she wanted him at her beck and call and that's exactly what happened. He was like a dog on a chain." Sewell was murdered in her lunch hour minutes after making secret arrangements to meet someone who was not her husband in the graveyard in Bakewell. Downing was arrested, interrogated without a solicitor and persuaded to sign a statement he could not read. Despite immediately retracting his confession, the intellectually backward Downing was found guilty. He served 27 years because he refused to admit guilt.

'"All the prison officers knew Stephen was innocent. They were begging him to just say he had done it so they could release him," said Hale. It was 22 years after his arrest that Smith, a self-styled psychic who became friends with Downing's mother and sister, asked Hale if she could help him uncover the truth behind Sewell's murder. Smith correctly said Wendy had been attacked in one place and moved to another, and had been choked, perhaps with a pair of tights. She also gave the initials of the man she claimed was the murderer.

'"These were interesting details but none of it was rocket science," said Hale. Back in his cell, however, Downing was impressed. "When my family first mentioned Christine, I imagined a warty old crone with a black cloak and a pointy hat," he said shortly after his release. "I was amazed to see this glamorous creature in a photo. I asked my family for her address and wrote to her immediately." The two began exchanging letters. "We wrote about anything and everything," Smith has said. "In later years they often became quite passionate. In effect, we were having a romance by letter." Although Downing told his family he was falling in love with Smith, her behaviour confused them: she refused to accompany them on prison visits and told them she was not interested in romance. "She didn't know Stephen showed me the letters she wrote him," said Hale. "They were pretty steamy, encouraging him to reply in kind and send her night clothes bought via the prison's mail-order business. He didn't have any money but he sent her what she asked for because he loved her." [This is not true. I didn't show Hale any letters and nor did I buy her any night clothes. The prison did not have a mail-order service]. Hale was concerned she might be keener on the publicity than the romance. The friendship between Smith and the family began to cool but Downing was infatuated and, when he was released on bail in February 2001, believed he was on the verge of marriage.

'Smith was determined not to let her quarry escape. "She hounded him with telephone calls," said Hale. Smith became impatient when Downing's compensation payments failed to materialise. She approached Hale in April with a tape she had secretly made of a telephone conversation they had had during the last months of Downing's imprisonment. "She hinted that it proved Stephen's guilt but never let me hear it and never took it to the police, even though I encouraged her to," said Hale.

"She took it to the newspapers but no one was interested." Smith took Downing to magazine offices to talk about their love but Hale had told Downing's parents about the tape and they turned to the press to accuse Smith of being a gold-digger. [Christine did not take me to any magazines: I was approached by a number of newspapers].

'Furious, Downing walked out on his parents in March, intending to move in with Smith. "But she wouldn't have him," said Hale. In the absence of any compensation money, the relationship continued to deteriorate: already a heavy drinker, Smith encouraged Downing to follow suit. He gave up his job in a restaurant and, despite training to be a security guard, failed to apply for a job. [I did two days training as a security guard but chose to leave as I didn't like the way the company operated]. Then last month, Smith was arrested for drink-driving with Downing beside her. [I wasn't with her when she was arrested: she'd already dropped me off]. She was banned for 11 months and fined £200. "Stephen was desperately upset and turned to his parents," said Hale. "She told him to choose between his family and her. He tried to keep in touch with both sides but she would not have it." Last week Smith offered a Sunday newspaper a tape of a conversation between her and Downing drunkenly arguing in the early hours, in which she claimed he admitted committing the murder. The paper refused the tape and instead, Smith took it to the police, who have sent it for transcription. "Of course, it isn't true," said Downing. "She was on and on at me to admit I killed Wendy Sewell and I just blurted it out. I thought she loved me; God knows why she's done this to me. I honestly thought she was my soulmate but now I realise everyone was right about her and I was wrong." [This is incorrect. I didn't "admit" to killing Wendy. I said: "If it makes you happy to believe I did it then so be it."]

'Hale is confident the tape will be dismissed by the police. "The appeal court cleared him on conclusive evidence and the only thing I am worried about now is Stephen himself. When news about the compensation money came out, it was like a red rag to a bull."

The Sunday Telegraph 14 July 2002:

'Stephen Downing, whose conviction for murdering a woman in a Bakewell cemetery was overturned this year, has been accused of assaulting a woman in the street and stalking another. The two women have told a team of Derbyshire detectives reinvestigating the 1973 murder of Wendy Sewell that they were allegedly the subject of Mr Downing's unwanted attentions before the killing. Both have recently given formal statements detailing their experiences. One of them alleges she was attacked by the teenaged Downing in a street in Bakewell in 1971. She claims that she was pushed into a doorway from behind and threatened that if she resisted she would be hurt. She managed to escape from her attacker, who she alleges she recognised as Mr Downing, who lived near her. She made a complaint to the police at the time but Mr Downing, who was questioned about the allegation, is understood to have given an alibi. [The alibi was that one of the cadets had gone to the police and admitted to the offence, saying it was for a laugh. He was given a caution. All the cadets were questioned]. The woman, who has asked not to be identified until the police reinvestigation is completed, told *The Telegraph*: "He pushed something in my back and said, 'Do as I tell you or I will hurt you'. I fought him off and when I told my husband what had happened he ran down the road looking for him but he was gone. I had got a good look at the person who attacked me. It was Stephen Downing and he was wearing an army cadet uniform. [I did not have a uniform as I hadn't been there long enough for one to be issued]. Although I had not been living in the area long, his family lived around the corner so I recognised him.

'"I told the police and they told me later that they had spoken to his parents. But they said there was nothing further they could do because someone had given him an alibi."

'The other woman, who has also asked for her identity to be protected, claims Mr Downing followed her home after work, some months before the attack on Mrs Sewell, a 32-year-old secretary, in September 1973. She said: "He followed me around more than a dozen times during a three-month period that spring. I was 19 at the time. Downing had a crush on me but I didn't like the way he went about showing it. He was really creepy, following me after work, walking at a distance behind me. One night I even hid in the toilets in the Market Place to avoid him. I did not want him following me home. I was also sent notes asking me to go out with him. I knew Wendy and when she was murdered so brutally it sent shivers down my spine… ." [I have never followed anyone home and I'm unaware of anyone making this claim.]

'Last May, this newspaper revealed that the inquiry team had been handed a tape of a conversation between Mr Downing and Christine Smith, his former girlfriend, since his release, in which he admitted to having carried out the murder. He has since said he claimed he was guilty only of testing Miss Smith's love for him. Last week, *The Telegraph* also revealed that Mr Downing allegedly made obscene telephone calls to women from prison. [I never made any obscene phone calls.] Josie Fisher, a solicitor's receptionist, has told police of how Mr Downing would allegedly pester her with disgusting suggestions. A spokesman for Derbyshire police said: "We cannot comment on the inquiry as it is still ongoing."'

The Observer Sunday, 21 July 2002:

'Downing's mother is assaulted'

'Police were keeping an open mind yesterday over whether an attack on the mother of Stephen Downing was linked to her son, whose conviction for murdering a woman in a churchyard was quashed after he spent 27 years in jail. Juanita Downing was dragged out of her home in Bakewell. She was punched repeatedly and told, "Keep your mouth shut." Inspector Robin Gray said Mrs Downing answered a knock at the door of the home she shares with her husband, Ray, at about 8.15pm on Thursday. Her attacker dragged her down the steps of the house and punched her several times before fleeing on foot. She was treated at the scene by medical staff, but did not need to go to hospital.

'Insp Gray said: "We believe that the only connection to Mr Downing is the fact that this attack happened at his parents' house. We are keeping an open mind over any connection to the murder of Wendy Sewell." He appealed for witnesses. The only description of the assailant is that he wore blue jeans and a dark top. Speaking from the family home, Stephen Downing said his mother was very shaken: "She is in quite a bad way." Neighbours said they were shocked. Avril Prime, 59, said: "I went to see her as soon as I heard what had happened. She was in a mess, very badly shaken up." Another neighbour, who declined to be named, said: "It's pretty shocking. This is a quiet area. You don't get things like that happening round here."' [My mother's attacker fled on the back of a motorcycle. At the time of the attack, my father and I were in a pub about two miles away].

After the Court of Appeal overturned my conviction, Derbyshire Police reinvestigated the murder under the name Operation Noble. In 2002, they interviewed 1,600 witnesses, at an estimated cost of £500,000 – though I myself declined to be re-interviewed. In February 2003, Derbyshire Police revealed the findings of their reinvestigation. There were twenty-two other possible suspects, many of whom had been suggested by Don Hale during his campaign and are named in his book *Town Without Pity*. All were ruled out. After failing to link any other person with the murder, and unable to eliminate me as the suspect, they declared the case closed. Even though I remained the prime suspect, the 'double jeopardy' rule meant the police did not submit the results of their inquiries to the Crown Prosecution Service as I cannot be re-arrested and charged with the same crime without new evidence.

The report called on Derbyshire Police to apologize and explain their actions, which had been highlighted at appeal in 2002 as 'substantially and significantly breaching the Judges' Rules.' They were asked to explain this recent finding and confirm why crucial evidence had been deliberately kept from the defence. Campaigning editor, Don Hale, had been told by police that all the evidence had been 'burnt, lost and destroyed'. When the murder weapon, a pickaxe handle was found to be on display at Derby Museum it was subjected to a modern forensic examination. My fingerprints were not found and there was a bloody palm print from an as yet unidentified person.

That same month, Derbyshire Police published the following extracts of Operation Noble on their website:

'In order to allay further speculation arising from recent press articles regarding the results of the re-investigation into the murder of Wendy Sewell in Bakewell in 1973, Derbyshire police have announced that they are not looking for any other person.

'Police launched a re-investigation into the case in April 2002 after the Court of Appeal quashed the murder conviction of Stephen Downing in January that year, on the grounds that the conviction was unsafe. Derbyshire's Deputy Chief Constable Bob Wood said: "Wendy Sewell was a young woman in the prime of her life who was robbed of her future as a result of a vicious attack. We have carried out an extremely thorough re-investigation and have been able to eliminate 22 individuals from the enquiry. Despite the lengthy investigation we have not been able to eliminate Stephen Downing from the enquiry. We acknowledge that mistakes, relating to the Judges' Rules in place at the time, were made in the original investigation."

'The re-investigation was carried out by Derbyshire Constabulary led by Detective Chief Superintendent David Gee and overseen by an independent advisory group. This comprised a representative from the Crown Prosecution Service; a senior barrister, who has an extensive background in criminal cases; a recently retired Senior Investigating Officer from another police force, who was the major crime advisor to the Stephen Lawrence enquiry; and Stephen Downing's media advisor. [Wendy Sewell's widower David was also on the panel but I was not allowed on and much of what was discussed was kept from me by my lawyer due to the panel's confidentiality agreement].

'The advisory group is now considering its own independent findings and a report is expected in the near future, when a further press conference will be held. During the six month investigation 16 officers re-interviewed all the surviving witnesses, except Stephen Downing; made house to house enquiries; interviewed new witnesses; and worked with Don Hale, the former editor of the *Matlock Mercury* who had campaigned for the freedom of Stephen Downing.

'Mr Wood explained the reason for not interviewing Stephen Downing. "Throughout our enquiry our officers have had a good working relationship with Mr Downing. He provided us with his fingerprints for elimination purposes but on the advice of his lawyers declined to be formally interviewed.

'"Under English law the police are unable to compel Mr Downing to give an interview in these circumstances. But I want to stress that Mr Downing had every right to take that decision."

'In all, officers completed 2,000 lines of enquiry, examined 2,600 files and documents and traced and interviewed 360 new witnesses. All of the surviving witnesses were re-interviewed and did not waver from their original statements. Forensic evidence was also reviewed as part of the reinvestigation. An independent forensic expert from Kent Police carried out blood pattern analysis and oversaw other forensic work that was necessary. Examination of the murder weapon, a pick axe handle, confirmed that the blood on it was that of Wendy Sewell. For several years the weapon was an exhibit in the police museum and had been handled by many people. Fingerprint analysis found a partial palm print and a partial fingerprint. Neither of these prints compare with any given by anyone subject of the re-investigation. It is possible they could belong to someone who has handled it since.

'Mr Hale has given the police every piece of information he holds and all his notes of interviews. Documents from the courts, Ray Downing and the defence solicitors, were analysed. Mr Hales' book *A Town without Pity* was analysed line by line for evidence.

'Close examination of these documents has thrown up a number of anomalies.

'Three examples of how officers have been able to clarify some assertions made in *A Town without Pity* are:

- The speculation that Mrs Sewell was meeting a lover is incorrect. Officers have found a new witness who spoke to Mrs Sewell at 11.30 on the morning she died. Mrs Sewell told her she was going to visit the cemetery to look at headstones for her father's grave. This account is consistent with the statement of Mrs Sewell's mother taken at the time.
- Mr Hale draws significance to Mrs Sewell's missing bag and says her personal effects were never found. In fact the bag and her belongings were returned to Mr Sewell shortly after the murder.
- A number of witnesses to whom Mr Hale attributes personal comment have told officers they have never spoken to him. Many witnesses who recalled speaking to Mr Hale say his written version is not their recollection of what was said.
- At all stages of the investigation members of the Independent Advisory Group were consulted about the enquiry.
- When the enquiry was complete a file containing the names of 22 people was sent to the Crown Prosecution Service. A senior lawyer studied the file and advised that there was no evidence to link any of the 22 people, whose names have been put forward since the conviction of Stephen Downing, to the murder.
- The findings of the investigation confirm those of the Criminal Cases Review Commission back in November 2000. At that time they said, "The Commission considered all the evidence put before them. They decided that despite many assertions by Mr Downing's supporters that there may have been other possible suspects, none of their enquiries have given rise to sufficient new evidence to justify a reinvestigation."

'From a police perspective the case is now closed. All possible lines of enquiry have been exhausted. The case will only be re-opened if any substantial new evidence comes to light.'

Chris Clark's research pointed out that Operation Noble contradicts itself with regards to the pickaxe handle or 'exhibit'. First of all, it says I had handled it and then it goes on to say my fingerprints weren't on it. This must surely eliminate me from having handled it at any time. Also, there were six pickaxe handles, all stamped BUDC (Bakewell Urban District Council), which were stored in the workman's chapel.

**Derbyshire
Constabulary**

PUBLIC REPORT

OPERATION NOBLE

The Police Reinvestigation of the Murder of Wendy Sewell

in Bakewell, September 1973

February 2003

A SECOND LIFE SENTENCE

HISTORY OF THE CASE

The Initial Police Investigation

On 12 September 1973 at about 12.40 p.m. Wendy Sewell left her place of work at Catcliffe House, King Street, Bakewell and proceeded to walk up Butts Road towards Bakewell Cemetery. She was seen by a number of witnesses during her walk and one witness Charles Carman saw her enter the cemetery at about 12.50 p.m. that day.

Shortly afterwards Wendy Sewell was attacked in the cemetery. She had been struck a number of times to the head causing severe head injuries. In addition her trousers, pants, plimsolls and parts of her bra had been removed. These were found together with a bloodstained pickaxe handle close to the scene of the attack.

Stephen Downing a 17-year-old groundsman who had been working in the cemetery raised the alarm.

Stephen Downing was taken to Bakewell Police Station on 12 September 1973. Following questioning which lasted several hours he confessed to attacking Wendy Sewell and made a statement to this effect.

Wendy was taken to the Chesterfield Royal Hospital where on 14 September 1973 she died of the injuries she had sustained.

Stephen Downing's clothing, which was bloodstained, was seized and subjected to forensic examination. The forensic scientist, Norman Lee, provided evidence regarding the blood pattern on the clothing stating that it was a *"Textbook example .. which might be expected on the clothing of the assailant"*.

Stephen was subsequently charged with the murder of Wendy Sewell.

Stephen Downing's Trial

Stephen subsequently retracted his confession and pleaded not guilty at his trial, which took place at Nottingham Crown Court between 13 and 15 February 1974.

The two main points of the prosecution case were the confession and the forensic evidence. Of significance, Stephen Downing's defence chose not to challenge either the police observance of the Judge's Rules regarding the interview of suspects, nor the findings of the Forensic Scientist. This, despite the fact that at the time of going to trial the Defence were in possession of a separate specialist report that fundamentally challenged the findings of Norman Lee, the Forensic Scientist working on behalf of the Police.

There is no full transcript of the trial. However, in his summing up, the judge specifically referred to Stephen Downing's admission whilst giving evidence of having indecently assaulted Sewell. He now denies that he made those admissions during the trial.

Stephen Downing was found guilty by unanimous verdict. He was sentenced to be detained at Her Majesty's Pleasure.

Subsequent Court Proceedings

Stephen Downing applied for an extension of time within which to apply for leave to appeal and to call a new witness.

On 25 October 1974 the Court of Appeal heard the grounds for appeal.

A witness, who was 15 years of age at the time of the murder, claimed to have seen Stephen Downing leaving the cemetery at the same time she allegedly saw Wendy Sewell alive and unharmed.

The Appeal Court hearing on 25 October 1974 reached the conclusion that the evidence of her sighting Wendy Sewell walking towards the rear of the consecrated chapel was unreliable due to her line of sight being obstructed by mature trees. The Court refused leave to appeal against the conviction on the grounds that there was doubt about the credibility of any of her evidence.

As part of the re-investigation, this witness was re-interviewed and she was accompanied back to the cemetery. She reaffirmed that mature trees, which have since been felled, obstructed her line of sight. She also volunteered the fact that she is, and was at the time, short sighted.

The witness was unable to explain why she came forward with her original evidence.

The Campaign to Free Stephen Downing

The case generated considerable local and national publicity. The Downing family made extensive enquiries, enlisting the help of the then Editor of the Matlock Mercury, Mr. Don Hale. As a result of their campaigning and Stephens continued denial of committing the murder, the case was referred to the Criminal Cases Review Commission in 1997.

The Commission found there were grounds to refer the case back to the Court of Appeal.

On 15 January 2002 the Court of Appeal granted the appeal on the following grounds, namely: -

    a. That evidence of the interpretation of the blood staining, by the original forensic scientist could not be relied upon to support the conviction.

    b. That the trial was unsatisfactory by reason of the failure to challenge the admissibility of the confessions the appellant made.

At the Court of Appeal Lord Justice Pill in delivering the judgement of the Court stated:

"It is not, however, for this court to speculate as to what might have happened had the fundamental defect, which we find to have existed in the conduct of this case not been present.

As Lord Bingham had recently underlined in R v Pendleton [2002] 1 W.L.R,

"The question for its (the Court of Appeal's) consideration is whether the conviction is safe and not whether the accused is guilty".

In the somewhat bizarre circumstances of this case, we expressly do not address ourselves to the latter question."

Following the quashing of the conviction Don Hale's book " Town Without Pity" was published in which he speculated as to the possible identity of the killer of Wendy Sewell.

THE POLICE RE-INVESTIGATION

Following the decision of the Court of Appeal, the Chief Constable, Mr. David Coleman, decided that the circumstances of the original offence should be thoroughly re-investigated. This commenced on 15 April 2002.

The Deputy Chief Constable, Mr. Robert Wood, was to take overall responsibility for the re-investigation. A meeting was held involving Stephen Downing, his father Mr. Ray Downing, the former Editor of the Matlock Mercury, Mr. Don Hale, together with Stephen Downing's legal representative, to discuss and agree the way forward.

It was agreed all parties would have confidence in the Derbyshire Constabulary conducting the re-investigation, overseen by an Independent Advisory Group. The reasons being, the passage of time since the crime was committed, the fact that no officer involved in the original investigation was still serving and the benefit local knowledge would bring to the re-investigation.

The re-investigation would be headed by Detective Chief Superintendent David Gee and a team of experienced detectives working under an Independent Advisory Group that comprised:

1. A leading Criminal Cases barrister selected by the Downing family.
2. Stephen Downing's legal advisor.
3. A recently retired senior detective from an outside Force who was also Major Crime Advisor to the Stephen Lawrence enquiry.
4. An independent representative from the Crown Prosecution Service.

The ensuing re-investigation operated under the heading of 'Operation Noble'. Before the re-investigation could commence, it was necessary to convert existing manuscript data and statements onto the Home Office Large Major Enquiry System computerised database. Following completion of this process, a meeting was held with the Independent Advisory Group to decide upon the terms of reference for the re-investigation. These were:

> *"Examine and review all the available evidence and information relating to the death of Wendy Sewell on 14th September 1973. We will conduct any necessary further enquiries to establish who may, or may not, be responsible for the death of Wendy Sewell."*

The re-investigation, involving a team of 16 officers and staff took 6 months from April 2002 to October 2002. Subsequently an advice file was submitted to the Crown Prosecution Service, seeking their views as to the merits of proceeding against any of the identified individuals.

Detail of the Re-investigation

The methodology undertaken included:

- Public appeal for new information
- House to house enquiries in the area of the cemetery and Butts Road in Bakewell
- Re-interview of all surviving witnesses
- Interview of new witnesses
- Page by page analysis of the Don Hale publication entitled 'A Town without Pity'

- Complete forensic review and a re-examination of key exhibits
- Analysis of documentation supplied by the Courts, Don Hale, Ray Downing and the Defence solicitors
- Analysis of anonymous letters received prior to the re-investigation

In order to create the best environment for officers to elicit information from potential witnesses, it was necessary to refresh their skills in the cognitive interview process. This technique enables interviewing officers to elicit the maximum amount of memory recall through psychologically based processes. This proved to be of undoubted benefit throughout the re-investigation. The volume of work generated during the re-investigation is best evidenced by referral to the below statistics:

- 2,000 lines of enquiry have been completed
- 2,600 documents and files have been examined
- 1,300 named individuals have been entered into the nominal database
- 360 new witnesses have been traced and interviewed
- 245 new witness statements obtained

All surviving witnesses have been re-interviewed and re-affirmed the evidence in their original statements and given at Stephen Downings trial .

"TOWN WITHOUT PITY" BY DON HALE

Prior to and during the re-investigation, a considerable amount of police time has been spent with Mr. Don Hale, the former Editor of the Matlock Mercury newspaper and author of "Town Without Pity", the book, based on his research into the murder of Wendy Sewell.

Mr. Hale acknowledges that there are no other records or information that he can provide to the re-investigation. Mr. Hale has been fully co-operative throughout the re-investigation process. However, there are a number of anomalies contained within Mr. Hale's documentation, and within "Town Without Pity", that, taken in isolation, have the potential to detract the reader from the facts surrounding the case.

The following are significant examples, which carry less weight when subjected to scrutiny:

1. There has been much speculation that Wendy Sewell went to the cemetery for a pre-arranged meeting with an unknown lover and it was he that attacked her. The re-investigation located a witness who had spoken to Wendy Sewell at 11.30 am in her office on the morning of her attack. This witness told of her conversation and Wendy's intention to visit the cemetery that lunchtime to look at different styles of headstones for her fathers grave. This is consistent with Wendy's mother's account in 1973 of the both of them wanting to erect a memorial on the unmarked grave in Sheffield.

2. Mr. Hale draws significance to the missing bag owned by Wendy Sewell and draws an inference of sinister connotations when, in fact, the possessions in question had been returned to David Sewell shortly after the commission of the offence. Furthermore, Mr Hale alleges that none of Wendy's personal effects were ever traced. This is clearly at odds with the facts.

3. A number of witnesses to whom Mr. Hale attributes personal comment and testimony when interviewed deny ever speaking to him. Many of the witnesses who did recall speaking with him say that Mr. Hale's version of events as written is not their recollection of conversations that took place.

A SECOND LIFE SENTENCE

FORENSIC REVIEW

Following a thorough review of the available material and previous forensic reports, the re-investigation team embarked upon a comprehensive examination of all available exhibits that were likely to assist with identifying who was responsible for the murder of Wendy Sewell It was decided that it was necessary for the work to be carried out as independently of any previous examinations as possible. Mr. J. Fraser, Head of Kent Police Forensic Investigation, was commissioned to carry out the blood pattern analysis work and advise upon and oversee any other examinations that were necessary. The work carried out and results are summarised below.

Scene

Mr. Fraser examined the scene plan and photographs in an effort to determine the nature of the attack upon Wendy Sewell. His conclusions give a slightly more informative picture of the attack but revealed no new evidence.

Pick-Axe Handle

Since the conclusion of the trial process in 1974 the exhibit has been handled by numerous people and stored in less than ideal conditions. This has resulted in contamination.

Examination of this item concluded that the pattern of blood staining on it was characteristic of that caused by repeated blows to a bloodstained item.

DNA profiling of the weapon has been undertaken to confirm that the blood on the item is that of Wendy Sewell. No other DNA samples have been recovered from the pick axe handle. The blood staining was the only area of the exhibit suitable for DNA examination.

This exhibit was not subjected to fingerprint examination during the initial investigation. No reason for this decision has been revealed. However, it is feasible that this was a combination of:

The limited scientific opportunities available for such an item at that time
There was no doubt that it was the murder weapon.
Stephen Downing admitted the offence and to having handled the exhibit previously.

The item has now been subjected to a variety of tests to recover any fingerprints that may be present. The results of these are that a partial palm print has been identified. This has been compared against Stephen Downing and the other people subject of the enquiry with negative results. Because it is only a partial palm print, it is not possible to speculatively compare it against the database held on the NAFIS national computer. In addition, a partial fingerprint has also been found but this is not suitable for comparison. Neither of these latent marks can be dated and at the present time remain unidentified.

Blood Pattern Analysis of Clothing of Stephen Downing

Mr. Fraser examined the clothing, considered all previous forensic examinations and took into account the varying accounts offered by Stephen Downing since 1973, including those obtained at Bakewell Police Station on the day of the attack. His examination of these items detected a number of original blood stains not previously identified.

THE CASE OF STEPHEN DOWNING

CONCLUSION

The original trial defence team of Stephen Downing never challenged the circumstances under which Stephen made his admissions. The reason for this failure has not been established and was not within the remit of the re-investigation. It is accepted that there was a breach of the Judges' Rules and that the Police fell short of the required standard of the times.

The differing forensic opinions regarding blood distribution are an issue. The Police are not the appropriate body to drawn a final conclusion which would have been a matter for a court of law. The police re-investigation has been carried out under the scrutiny of a jointly agreed Independent Advisory Group (with the support of the Downing family and legal representatives) comprising respected individuals across the crime investigation arena. This group has accessed and scrutinised all of the available information and evidence generated by the re-investigation team.

In terms of the depth of the enquiry, the Crown Prosecution Service have commented on the thoroughness of the re-investigation.

Once the file had been forwarded to the Crown Prosecution Service its contents were scrutinised by a senior lawyer over a three month period. The advice from the CPS was that there is no evidence to link any of the individuals who since the conviction of Stephen Downing, have been the subject of speculation and innuendo in connection with the attack on Wendy Sewell on 12 September 1973.

The Criminal Case Review Commission in 1999 recommended the case to be referred to the Court of Appeal. Their lengthy investigation considered all the evidence and decided that despite the many assertions by Mr. Downing's supporters that there may have been other possible suspects, none of their enquiries had given rise to sufficient new evidence to justify a re-investigation. The findings of the Police re-investigation confirm those of the CCRC in 1999.

The Police are not looking for any other person for the murder of Wendy Sewell, a young woman in the prime of her life who was robbed of her future as a result of this vicious attack. All possible lines of enquiry have been exhausted. The case is now closed unless any substantial new evidence comes to light.

R J Wood, OBE, QPM
Deputy Chief Constable

Pick-Axe Handle

Since the conclusion of the trial process in 1974 the exhibit has been handled by numerous people and stored in less than ideal conditions. This has resulted in contamination.

Examination of this item concluded that the pattern of blood staining on it was characteristic of that caused by repeated blows to a bloodstained item.

DNA profiling of the weapon has been undertaken to confirm that the blood on the item is that of Wendy Sewell. No other DNA samples have been recovered from the pick axe handle. The blood staining was the only area of the exhibit suitable for DNA examination.

This exhibit was not subjected to fingerprint examination during the initial investigation. No reason for this decision has been revealed. However, it is feasible that this was a combination of:

The limited scientific opportunities available for such an item at that time
There was no doubt that it was the murder weapon.
Stephen Downing admitted the offence and to having handled the exhibit previously.

The item has now been subjected to a variety of tests to recover any fingerprints that may be present. The results of these are that a partial palm print has been identified. This has been compared against Stephen Downing and the other people subject of the enquiry with negative results. Because it is only a partial palm print, it is not possible to speculatively compare it against the database held on the NAFIS national computer. In addition, a partial fingerprint has also been found but this is not suitable for comparison. Neither of these latent marks can be dated and at the present time remain unidentified.

The 'exhibit' does not have a BUDC stamp on and was brought into the cemetery by Wendy's attacker. Here is an extract from Operation Noble with contradictory statements underlined by Chris Clark:

My MP, Patrick McLoughlin, brought Operation Noble up in Parliament in reference to the Criminal Justice Bill and suggested Home Secretary David Blunkett asked other police forces to re-examine old cases to avoid other miscarriages of justice. This extract is from *Hansard*, the transcripts of Parliamentary debates:

'Criminal Justice Bill HC Deb 04 December 2002 vol 395 cc912-92 912 [Relevant document: The Second Report from the Home Affairs Committee, Session 2002–03, on the Criminal Justice Bill (HC 83).] Order for Second Reading read.

'Mr. Patrick McLoughlin (West Derbyshire). "Serious cases of miscarriage of justice have done much to damage the criminal justice system. During consideration of the Bill, I ask the Home Secretary to examine the operation that was set up by the Derbyshire constabulary – it was 916 called Operation Noble – in the reinvestigation of the Wendy Sewell murder, following the release of Stephen Downing about 27 years after being convicted, the conviction having been found unsafe by the Court of Appeal. Will the right hon. Gentleman take it from me that Operation Noble has been far sighted and has enabled the chief constable to reinvestigate a serious crime, involving all those who were concerned in the case? Operation Noble should be examined by other police forces throughout the country."

'Mr. Blunkett. "We would all be pleased to learn lessons from that operation and to reflect on improvements. It is not often that I pay tribute to a measure that was enacted under Baroness Thatcher's notorious reign."

'Mr. McLoughlin. "Go on."

'Mr. Blunkett. "I will go on. I shall dip a toe in hot water. By 1984, it had been recognised by everyone that there were major problems. The Police and Criminal Evidence Act 1984 and the development of the PACE code since have been important and welcomed by everyone. We need to build upon that in a sensitive way. We are not sweeping that aside in introducing the Bill. We need to be able to enhance and modernise a learning experience over the past 18 years. I welcome the way in which the Derbyshire police have approached the Downing case."'

Daily Mail 2003:

'Fateful stroll which led to murder'

'Before she left her Bakewell office on a bright lunchtime in September 1973, Wendy Sewell left a note for colleagues saying she was nipping out for a breath of fresh air. [No note was ever discovered or handed to police]. The Forestry Commission typist, who was 32, lived a few miles away in a large farmhouse with her husband David in the Derbyshire Dales village of Middleton-by-Youlgreave. He had left home at about 6am that morning, setting off for work in Derby, and had not woken his wife.

'After his wife left her office in the Derbyshire market town on September 12 for a stroll to the nearby cemetery, neither Mr Sewell nor Wendy's work colleagues would see her alive again. Mrs Sewell told a friend she was going to the site to look at headstones, but was later discovered savagely beaten and partially clothed among the graves. She remained conscious, and Stephen Downing, a 17-year-old groundsman, claimed to have discovered her body.

'He worked for the local council tending the graveyard less than half a mile from his home. Finding her body Mr Downing said that he had been the first person to come across the woman, finding her in a pool of blood, before raising the alarm at about 1.20pm. After a police officer arrived at the scene, Wendy staggered to her feet, stumbled and then fell, hitting her head against a gravestone. She was taken to Chesterfield Royal Hospital, but died two days later as a result of the terrible injuries she had received from multiple blows with a pickaxe handle. She had been unable to name her attacker.

'Mr Downing, who had a reading age of 11, was arrested at the scene and found to have blood on his clothing and access to a pickaxe handle. The teenager was taken to Bakewell police station where he was questioned for eight hours and later admitted to attacking and sexually assaulting Mrs Sewell. He said that he had exposed her breasts as he was attempting to check for a heartbeat, but admitted that he had also indecently touched her as she lay injured on the ground. [I did not admit to this, only to placing my hands between her breasts to check for a heartbeat]. Mr Downing signed a confession and when she died in hospital, he was formally charged with her murder.

'A Court of Appeal hearing last year accepted that he had not been formally cautioned until late that night and that he had not been informed of his right to have a solicitor present. Supporters of Mr Downing have claimed that parts of his confession were suggested to him by officers, an allegation denied by police. Thirteen days later, Mr Downing retracted the confession that he had been responsible for the attack. On February 13, 1974, at Nottingham Crown Court, he was found guilty of murder and sentenced to be detained at Her Majesty's Pleasure, with the trial judge recommending a minimum term of 17 years.

'Before he was taken down, the judge told Stephen: "You have been convicted on the clearest evidence of the offence." But his parents Ray Downing, then a local bus driver, and

Juanita Downing disagreed. Following their son's arrest they hired a private detective to make inquiries about the killing. They were unhappy that Mrs Sewell had been portrayed in court as a happily married woman, when it was known that she had had an affair. She had had an affair in 1967 with local man John Marshall, leaving her husband and giving birth to her lover's child in 1968. The infant was later adopted and Mrs Sewell returned to her husband in 1971, moving with him to Middleton-by-Youlgreave. Private detective Robert Erwin, of Clowne, Derbyshire, conducted interviews on the Downing family's behalf in which he claimed witnesses said they had seen a man running away from the murder scene.

'He sent submissions to the Home Secretary and Mr Downing's solicitors also appealed against his conviction. They referred to a 15-year-old witness who claimed to have seen Mr Downing leaving the cemetery at the same time she had seen Wendy Sewell alive and unharmed. At a hearing on 25 October 1974, the Appeal Court concluded that the new evidence was unreliable and refused leave to appeal against the conviction. Unbowed, Mr Downing's family continued to maintain that he was innocent and the prisoner also made consistent denials to the parole board, which deemed him "in denial of murder" and unsuitable for release.

'The Court of Appeal hearing in 2002 heard that he made three confessions to the killing in conversations with prison doctors. In 1994, the Downing family enlisted the help of local newspaper editor Don Hale after a chance meeting with Ray Downing, then working as a taxi driver. A new campaign to urge authorities to review the case began, with regular articles in Mr Hale's weekly newspaper, the *Matlock Mercury*, and in national publications.

'Mr Hale, who later won an OBE and press awards for his work, claimed that there were a number of inconsistencies in the evidence used to convict Mr Downing and said that new witnesses had provided him with proof that someone else was behind the killing.

'In 1996, West Derbyshire MP Patrick McLoughlin visited the Home Office to discuss the case, but that October Mr Downing failed to gain parole and lost a High Court appeal for an early parole hearing. With the Downing family, Mr Hale continued to lobby MPs and police and the case was referred to the Criminal Cases Review Commission (CCRC) in November 1997.

'In 2000, Mr Downing was awarded £500 in an out-of-court settlement at the European Court of Human Rights, after he claimed he had not been given the opportunity to contest his continued detention.

'As Mr Downing continued to serve his sentence, the CCRC considered the new evidence, including DNA analysis of the murder weapon and a file provided by the campaign team.

'He was eventually freed on bail on February 7 last year, leaving his cell at Littlehey Prison, in Cambridgeshire. Mr Downing said at the time: "I know a lot has changed, but I have kept in touch with what is going on in the world by reading newspapers and listening to the radio and from letters, phone calls and visits. There is so much I want to do. For a start I want to buy a mobile phone – they weren't even dreamed of when I came in here."

'He returned home to Bakewell and undertook to working as a commis chef at Aitch's Wine Bar and Bistro. In Bakewell, a woman attacked Mr Downing, alleging that he had been responsible for an assault on her mother before Mrs Sewell's killing. Police arrested the woman, but no formal charges were brought against her. Employer, John Hattersley, had called the police and insisted that the woman was arrested and he would call into the police station the following day to make a statement.

'Less than a year after his release, on January 15, 2002, three judges at the Court of Appeal ruled on his case. They declared that the conviction was "unsafe", but stopped short of declaring him innocent.

'Mr Downing is reported to have already received about £250,000 in compensation for his time spent in custody and the final sum is expected to be between £500,000 and £1.8 million. The Home Office has refused to disclose the exact amount of money Mr Downing will receive.

'Almost 30 years after Mrs Sewell took her fateful lunchtime stroll, the community of Bakewell hopes those findings will allow the town to finally leave behind its most infamous afternoon.'

The compensation I received was nowhere near the figure bandied around in the press but I am not revealing the exact amount. It was enough for me to buy a house and give my parents something to compensate for the time and money they spent visiting me for twenty-seven years and campaigning for my release.

The Sunday Telegraph, 16 March 2003:

'Downing tries to hire women for nude photoshoots'

'Stephen Downing, the only suspect for the murder of a Bakewell woman 30 years ago, has set himself up as a "glamour" photographer and is inviting models to nude photoshoots at his home. Downing, who served 27 years for the sexually-motivated killing of Wendy Sewell before his conviction was quashed last year, told an undercover reporter posing as a model that he wanted to photograph her both at his home and outdoors, either naked or wearing provocative lingerie.

'He also invited her to stay overnight with him and offered to pay her and take her out to dinner. Downing did not, however, inform her of his murder conviction – which was overturned on appeal – or that an extensive police reinvestigation of the killing found that he remained the only viable suspect.

'The police reinvestigation also heard that Downing had confessed repeatedly since being released from prison. His father, Ray, told the police that his son had admitted killing Mrs Sewell. Christine Smith, Downing's former girlfriend, also taped him confessing to the killing.

'The inquiry heard additional claims that Downing had stalked or assaulted at least three other women in Bakewell before Mrs Sewell's murder and that during his incarceration he made obscene phone calls to five others. An undercover reporter posing as a model contacted Downing via email after *The Telegraph* was informed that he was soliciting lingerie models on the internet. The reporter pretended to be "Jo", a 29-year-old from Lincolnshire who was interested in posing for glamour shots and who had heard that Downing was a photographer in this field.

'Within days Downing had replied, saying: "I am interested." During later emails, Downing said that he wanted to take pictures which would feature "plenty of lingerie". In another email he was more expansive, saying that he wanted to take glamour pictures to "broaden my horizons and increase my portfolio." He added: "The pictures I was looking to take for the portfolio were from portrait through to artistic nude. I would like to concentrate mostly on lingerie. I have got a few items of lingerie but it might be best if you brought your own and whatever you like best. I was going to have a model come up from Suffolk but she has had to cancel as her mother was taken ill and she and her sons were also getting over heavy colds. As for the outdoor poses, I was thinking of lingerie, topless and nude at a few discreet locations. Naturally if the weather was not favourable then I would not want to go out either.

"'I would like to set up a commercial studio but for now I will have to make do with a spare bedroom," he says. In response to Jo's question, he adds: "I was not proposing to have anyone else present." Downing then volunteers: "I have got a spare room if you wanted to stay over and I am happy to take you to a fine restaurant for lunch (and dinner if you are staying over)."

'Downing, who lives on his own in a house in Bakewell, added his personal contact details but stressed that he was "not looking to do anything pornographic", insisting: "I would not expect a model to do anything she was not entirely comfortable with." He boasted: "If you are familiar with the work of Patrick Lichfield and David Bailey then it will give you a rough idea of what I am trying to emulate."

'David Sewell, the widower of Wendy Sewell, said that Downing's desire to photograph naked women at his home was a worry. "He clearly has a reputation so it is a matter of some concern." Mr Downing yesterday declined to comment.'

This article is not correct – I did not invite models to nude photoshoots. I was also fed up with the constant references in the press to sexual assaults on Wendy Sewell. It was proven forensically that she was not sexually assaulted.

Daily Mirror, 26 March 2008:

'After spending 27 years in prison Stephen Downing is obsessed by being a copper'

'He was scarred after spending 27 years in jail for a murder he was eventually cleared of committing. Since his release on a technicality Stephen Downing has made no secret of his resentment at the officers who put him behind bars. Yet bizarrely the social misfit seems to have become obsessed with acting and dressing like a copper. He has bought ex-police jackets on the internet, visited eBay sites that flog handcuffs and contacted websites that offer police caps and badges. He has also snapped up police keyrings from foreign forces.

'Last week he was seen leaving home in a four-wheel drive Isuzu Trooper equipped with strobe lights normally seen on the roof of emergency vehicles. Bachelor Downing, 52, also wears a fluorescent jacket, black trousers, white shirt and black boots as he drives to visit his elderly parents Ray and Juanita. They live just a stone's throw from the cemetery in Bakewell, Derbyshire, where typist Wendy Sewell, 34 [*sic*], was found bludgeoned to death in 1973. After being sensationally cleared of her murder in 2001, Downing returned to the town, using his £500,000 compensation to move into a smart yellow stone-brick semi.

'But his obsession with police memorabilia has recently begun to raise eyebrows. One resident said: "He has started to look like a copper. If you see him in his four-wheel drive you'd swear he was someone official." The elderly man, who asked not to be named, added: "He wears the yellow jacket even when it's hot. It is all very weird." It is believed police were alerted some time ago to Downing's strange behaviour. One item he bought was a blue police fleece from a site called The One Stop Cop Shop. By law it was sold without badges, but still had distinctive blue and white check strapping, radio loops and epaulettes.

'A police source said: "People have to be very careful if they're selling ex-police merchandise. As long as they are de-badged it is fine for people to wear them. But impersonating a police officer is a very serious crime." Downing broke his silence two years ago when he said life had been "cruel" since his release. He said: "I can't get work anywhere. Whether that's to do with my past I don't know."

'Downing, who has always maintained his innocence, was asked about his new "hobby". He snapped: "Who told you about it? If you don't tell me who told you I'm saying nothing. Why should I say anything?"'

I did buy some police memorabilia but it was mostly American with proceeds from the sales going to the 11 September fund following the attack on the Twin Towers. Following this article, I wonder if I was set up for what followed a month or so later, which is detailed here.

Mirror.co.uk, 30 May 2008:

'Stephen Downing in bogus cop quiz'

'The man freed over the Bakewell Tart murder case has been arrested for allegedly impersonating a police officer. Loner Stephen Downing, 52, was quizzed by cops following revelations in the *Mirror* in March. He was interviewed at his local police station in Bakewell, Derbyshire and freed on bail pending further inquiries. Bachelor Downing spent 27 years in jail…before being cleared on a technicality in 2001 and receiving an estimated £500,000 compensation. We revealed how neighbours became concerned when he began dressing like a PC after buying ex police gear on the internet.'

Derbyshire Telegraph October 13, 2008:

'A Derbyshire man who had a murder conviction quashed after 27 years in prison has been found guilty of giving the impression of being a police officer. Steven Downing, 52, of Milford, Bakewell, had denied entering the Aldi store, in Station Road, Buxton, on February 16, wearing an item of clothing similar to that of a police uniform which was calculated to deceive a member of the public. Magistrates found Mr Downing guilty of the charge. He faces a fine of up to £1,000.

'A separate charge of impersonating a police officer was withdrawn at a previous hearing. High Peak Magistrates' Court, in Buxton, heard how Downing, who was convicted at Nottingham Crown Court in 1974 for the murder of Wendy Sewell the previous year, had entered the shop wearing the uniform on February 16.

'John Cooper, prosecuting, said the defendant attempted to buy four packs of shandy but staff refused to serve him alcohol on the basis they believed he was an on-duty police officer. He was wearing what appeared to be a black police jacket with a chequered strip around it, which had the words "Photographix" emblazoned on the back. He also wore a pin badge with the words "Derbyshire Constabulary Armed Response Vehicle unit" on it, as well as black trousers and black shoes.

'When service was refused, Downing called the police and officers attended the scene. He was subsequently arrested and charged. At today's hearing, shop manager Mark Strickland said: "At the time of the incident, I was in the office talking with the area manager when I was alerted by a cashier who said she had refused service of alcohol to a man who was dressed in what looked to be a police uniform. Visually, at first, it seemed like a police officer." But giving evidence in his defence, Downing, who said he was working as a freelance photographer at the time, said: "I bought the jacket from an internet website because it was durable and ideal for business purposes and I wanted to advertise my company name 'Photographix'. I did not want people believing it was an article of police uniform."

'Asked about the badge, he said: "I do have a collection of police badges, between 50 and 60, all bought from the internet, most of them covering American states and one or two British ones."

'Downing was fined £437, and ordered to pay costs of £650 and a victim surcharge of £15.'

Contrary to what this article says, I was not arrested but invited to a meeting with Buxton police at their headquarters. They charged me with impersonating a police officer and the magistrates' court gave me a fine. When I appealed to the crown court, I was acquitted, which speaks for itself.

Chapter 14

Light at the End of the Tunnel

Derbyshire Times, 28 October 2009:

'Fresh claim in Wendy Sewell murder case'

'The unknown killer of Wendy Sewell in Bakewell Cemetery in 1973 may have murdered a teenager earlier that year, according to a new book. Crime writer Scott Lomax – who makes the claim in his book *Unsolved Murders In And Around Derbyshire* – wants detectives to probe a link between Mrs Sewell's murder and the killing of 14-year-old Judith Roberts in Tamworth in 1972. Bakewell man Stephen Downing served 27 years in prison for Mrs Sewell's murder. His conviction was quashed in 2002 after a campaign led by former *Mercury* editor Don Hale, who argued whoever killed Mrs Sewell also raped and killed hitchhiker Barbara Mayo near Glapwell in 1970.

'But Mr Lomax, from Brimington, said: "I do not believe Wendy was killed by Barbara Mayo's murderer. Whilst there are some similarities there are also major differences. I believe police should be looking at a link between the murders of Wendy Sewell and Judith Roberts. Both women were struck repeatedly around the head and both women were partially stripped, but no evidence of sexual assault was present in either case."

'Andrew Evans was convicted of Judith Roberts' murder, before the Court of Appeal ruled his confession was unreliable and cleared him. Mr Lomax added: "The police never considered a link at the time because by the time of Wendy Sewell's murder, Andrew Evans was in prison having confessed to Judith Roberts' death. But like

Stephen Downing, he had given a confession for a crime he did not commit. I believe the police should now be looking at whether there are two killers in these cases or just one man who has so far evaded justice."

'Derbyshire Constabulary's Operation Noble reinvestigated the murder after Mr Downing's release, but none of the 22 other suspects were charged. No-one from Derbyshire Constabulary was available to comment on Mr Lomax's claims.'

It would take another four years before this link was raised again by former police intelligence officer Chris Clark who then contacted Derbyshire Police. He made a freedom of information (FOI) request and asked for a copy of Wendy Sewell's pathology report and copies of the statements from all the people, including myself, who had found her in Bakewell Cemetery. On 25 July 2013 Derbyshire Police FOI responded:

'Dear Mr Clark. FREEDOM OF INFORMATION REQUEST - REFERENCE NO: 001624/13 I write in connection with your request for information which was received by Derbyshire Constabulary on 11/07/2013. I note you seek access to the following information: "I am asking for a copy of the pathology report on Wendy Sewell 12.9.1973 Bakewell & witness statements from the people (including Stephen Downing) who found her in Bakewell Cemetery."

'Result of Searches: Following receipt of your request, searches were conducted within Derbyshire Constabulary to locate any relevant information. The searches located information relevant to your request. Decision: I have today decided not to disclose the located information to you as I am claiming exemptions under Sections Section 30(1)(a) (b)(c) - Investigations and proceedings conducted by public authorities and Section 40(2) - Personal information of the Freedom of Information Act 2000; the rationales for which are shown below. Therefore please accept this letter as a formal refusal of your request.

'Refusal of Request – Section 17 Section 17(1) provides that - A public authority which, in relation to any request for information, is to any extent relying on a claim that any provision of Part II relating to the duty to confirm or deny is relevant to the request or on a claim that information is exempt information must, within the time for complying with section 1(1), give the applicant a notice which – States that fact, Specifies the exemption in question, and States (if that would not otherwise be apparent) why the exemption applies.

'Wendy Sewell's body was found shortly after 12.50 p.m. on 12 September 1973 in Bakewell Cemetery having been struck a number of times to the head causing severe head injuries. Wendy was taken to the Chesterfield Royal Hospital where she died from the injuries on 14 September 1973. Stephen Downing, a 17 year old grounds man who has been working in the cemetery raised the alarm prior to being taken to Bakewell Police Station where he was questioned for several hours about the incident. During this questioning Stephen confessed to attacking Wendy. Following Wendy's death Stephen was charged with her murder and pleaded not guilty at this trial which took place at Nottingham Crown Court between 13 and 15 February 1974. Stephen was found guilty and sentenced to be detained at Her Majesty's Pleasure. Stephen applied for an extension of time within which to apply for leave to appeal and to call a new witness. The Court refused leave to appeal against conviction. The case was referred to the Criminal Cases Review Commission in 1997 who found grounds to refer it back to the Court of Appeal. On 15 January 2002 the Court of Appeal granted the appeal quashing the conviction. Following the Court of Appeal, the Chief Constable (David Coleman) decided that the circumstances of the original offence should be thoroughly re-investigated. This reinvestigation took 6 months from its commencement date to October 2002 following which an advice file was subsequently submitted to the Crown Prosecution Service. The police are not looking for any other person for the murder of Wendy Sewell and all possible lines of enquiry have been exhausted. Subsequently the case is now closed unless any substantial new evidence comes to light.

'Section 30 is a qualified, class-based exemption. Therefore in order for it to be engaged there is no need for a public authority to demonstrate any prejudice should the requested information be disclosed. It must simply show that the information is held for the purposes specified in the relevant part of the exemption that has been cited. This means that the public authority does not have to conduct a harm test but does need to conduct a public interest test.

'Section 30 For the purpose of the FOI request the FOI legislation states at Part VI, Section 62: - For the purposes of this Part, a record becomes a historical record at the end of the period of thirty years beginning with the year following that in which it was created.

'Where records created at different dates are for administrative purposes kept together in one file or other assembly, all the records in that file are to be treated for the purposes of this Part, as having been created when the latest of those records was created.

'This was echoed in the ACPO FOI Manual of Guidance Version 5 which was sanctioned by the ICO, it stated that "Information covered by Section 30 is subject to the 30 year rule, running from the date the last papers were added. This can be nothing more than an annotation on the front cover to say the file has been reviewed." Therefore it is the age of the information not the age of the investigation that is the key issue. Every time something is added to an investigation, the original record is changed, and the 30 years is reset. The ICO stated "Files containing numerous records (for example a murder case file) are treated as one record for this purpose and are 'created' when the last entry was made. Therefore, in theory a file could be 29 years old, have a record added to it in the 29th year and the clock would start again."

'Factors favouring disclosure for Section 30. Disclosure of the information would improve the public's knowledge and understanding of the investigatory process and, as all police investigations are publically funded, would show how public funds are being spent. The initial and subsequent investigation were highly emotive and attracted a large media/public interest but is now effectively finished, therefore disclosure of the information would show the public that the investigation had been conducted properly.

'Factors against disclosure for Section 30. Disclosure of the requested information would prejudice how investigations are carried out in the future as they would contain information about how the investigation was conducted. This would hinder the prevention and detection of crime and affect Derbyshire's law enforcement capabilities. Disclosure would inhibit the co-operation of witnesses to all crimes and undermine the partnership approach to investigations. Balance test: When balancing the public interest test I have to consider whether the information should be released in to the public domain. Competing arguments need to be weighed against each other especially as any disclosure under the Act is a disclosure to the world and not just the applicant.

'Whilst the proper detection, investigation and prosecution of crimes are cornerstones of a modern democratic society the Police Service will never divulge information if it will hinder those core responsibilities. Information released under the Act, where exemptions apply, will only be done where there is a tangible community benefit which is more powerful than the harm that can be done. I do not feel that this applies in this case. Consequently on balance, and from the harm evidenced above, I am of the view that the balance lies in favour of non-disclosure of the requested information.

'Section 40 is an absolute class-based exemption and a public authority is not obliged to conduct a prejudice test or a public interest test, but they must, however, show that one of the principles of fairness would be breached.

'Right to Request a Review (Complaint) Your attention is drawn to the attached sheet, which details your right of complaint. I would like to take this opportunity to thank you for your interest in Derbyshire Constabulary. Should you have any further enquiries concerning this matter, please write or contact the Freedom of Information Officer, on the above telephone number quoting the reference number in the header. Yours sincerely Kevin Lea Freedom of Information Officer.'

After receiving this rejected FOI request, Chris contacted me via my family for the first time.

Sunday Express 8 September 2013:

'After 40 years I'm prisoner to a murder I didn't commit'
'He is the victim of Britain's longest miscarriage of justice, but 40 years after he was "framed" for murder Stephen Downing says he is still a prisoner despite being a free man for more than a decade.

'Downing's world "turned upside down" on September 12, 1973, when he stumbled across Wendy Sewell's battered body in a graveyard. As a 17-year-old who could barely read and write, he was arrested and grilled for nine hours before being tricked into confessing to the attack in a statement written in pencil by the police. Two days later, the legal secretary, dubbed the "Bakewell Tart" due to her promiscuous lifestyle, died in hospital and he was charged with a murder that rocked the picturesque Derbyshire town.

'Now, four decades on, Downing is broke, single, and jobless and shunned by many. He revealed: "I might not be behind bars, but I'm still a prisoner. I lost half of my life serving a sentence for a crime I did not commit. Now I'm free but I've been left serving another sentence."

'He returned to his home town and by then he had received compensation – some reports put the figure as high as £750,000 but Downing disputes that sum. Since his release in 2001 he has spent money looking after loved ones but he blew thousands on others he claims were interested only in his money, while he also admits to acting like a "kiddie in a sweetshop" when it came to spending his cash. Now living on benefits, he fills his days gardening, watching TV and looking after his 80-year-old mother Juanita who has recently under-gone major surgery. "It's humiliating and pretty hopeless at the moment," admitted Downing, now 57. "What chance have I got at my age?"

'In recent years he has also had to cope with his father's death and psychic Christine Smith, Downing's former girlfriend, claiming to have taped him confessing to the killing. In 2004, his story was told in the BBC drama *In Denial Of M*urder in which Jason Watkins played Downing.

"'Some people still think I did it. It is just something I have to live with. In many ways life was easier inside – you did not have to look for a job, you got money, three meals a day and a roof over your head. Since I left prison things have been hard. I don't really have much of a life. Yes, I'm free but I am still paying for a crime I did not commit.'"

Despite this trial by media, friends, family and supporters were still standing up for me and trying to prove that I had nothing to do with the crime. On Tuesday, 26 November 2013 Chris Clark gave a live interview to BBC Radio Derbyshire outlining the miscarriage of justice meted out to me and said he thought the method and motive behind Wendy Sewell's attack and murder were identical to that of Peter Sutcliffe's, the Yorkshire Ripper.

On 2 December 2013 Chris was provided with a copy of the full pathologist report by my sister Chrissie via email. Chris replied to her the same day:

'Hello Chrissie, thank you so much for this. Did you hear the BBC Derby Radio broadcast? Julia Rodgerson of the *Derbyshire Times* is writing an article for Wednesday's paper. I made contact with Don Hale over the weekend and had a long chat. Keep in touch, I will keep you updated with progress made. If you haven't read it before, look up on Google anything you can find on the 1972 Judith Roberts murder where Andrew Evans was put away for 25 years! Another disgraceful miscarriage of justice with Peter Sutcliffe's MO [*modus operandi*] written all over it. Best Regards to You, Mum and Stephen. Your friend Chris.'

Having read the report, Chris then sent me, Don and Julia of the *Derbyshire Times* this email:

'Having passed a trained eye over the Pathologist Report I have reached the following conclusions. Wendy was originally attacked on the footpath by having a knotted garrotte looped over her neck and pulled tight in order to stupefy her, this would explain the massive bruise in the region of her "Adam's Apple" as well as the bruising to the deep cervical muscles in the back of her neck where the garrotte would be twisted in a tourniquet fashion. The result of this initial attack would have the effect of her dropping to her knees, where she was then rendered unconscious by repeated blows to the back of the head with the pick axe handle which we now know was brought to the scene by the offender, and not one from the workman's store. She was also repeatedly kicked.

'At that point she would have had her footwear removed and quickly stripped of her clothes from the waist down and her bra and top clothing pushed up to her shoulders (in a classic "Ripper" fashion to expose the torso ready for cutting/slashing/puncturing with knife and/or screwdriver). The offender then saw someone, most probably Stephen Downing, coming into the immediate vicinity and hid momentarily whilst Stephen went for help after seeing Wendy lying on the footpath. At this point Wendy would have been dragged from the initial site of attack which explains the findings of the bruising found on mouth, cheek, nose and ear all on left side; coupled with bruises found between her left knee and ankle. This is consistent with Wendy having been dragged by her left calf area from the original site of attack to the second area.

'All of this original pathology report was gone through together with 3 very senior police officers involved in the case present at the post-mortem and it beggars belief that it was not thought necessary by either The Prosecution or Defence to introduce the asphyxiation method at Stephen Downing's Trial, the later Appeal, or within "Operation Noble" in 2002; coupled with the fact of not finding what caused those asphyxiation injuries.'

Don Hale then responded to Chris:

'Hi Chris, thanks for the reports. Excellent analysis. Wendy was dragged or carried for about 30 yards from where she was first attacked. No explanation was offered. This is where she was seen by the workmen. If they had caught her she might still be alive. They shouted leave her and she fell and hit her head on a tombstone. All the anomalies were mentioned in my reports to the CCRC but the police have refused or were unable to answer. Some of the questions were included yesterday. Let's hope the DT [*Derbyshire Times*] will run with something. Do you think an appeal could be made to the Derbyshire Police Commissioner and/or to the IPCC [Independent Police Complaints Commission] over the poor reinvestigation? Thanks, Don.'

On 12 January 2014 Chris contacted Matthew Burton from BBC Radio Derby:

'Matthew. I do not want a rerun [of the] Radio Derby interview, but I thought that it was in the public interest of your listeners to bring to your attention the contents of the pathologist report. I currently do not know where the *Derbyshire Times* stands on this as they were the first to be provided with what is itself very damning evidence of the Derbyshire Police and Home Office Pathologist deliberately withholding vital evidence in Stephen Downing's 1974 Trial, his Autumn 1974 appeal, and his subsequent appeal and an orchestrated cover up by Derbyshire Police over many years including in "Operation Noble" of 2002. Best Regards Chris.'

On 11 January 2014 Chris emailed my MP, Patrick McLoughlin, who had been supportive during the campaign to free me just after the millennium:

'Dear Sir, my name is Chris Clark a retired police officer and I have been researching nationally 17 additional murders of women throughout the 1970s where I feel that owing to geographical profiling, the frenzied nature and method of attacks that Peter Sutcliffe was responsible for. In this list are 3 miscarriage of justice cases which involved Judith Roberts Wiggington/Tamworth 1972 Andrew Evans; Wendy Sewell

DAILY STAR SUNDAY, January 12, 2014

UK CRIME UNLIMI

■ EXCLUSIVE by ANDY GARDNER

EXPLOSIVE new evidence has come to light linking a notorious unsolved murder to the Yorkshire Ripper.

Retired detective Chris Clark has unearthed a rarely seen pathologist's report on murder victim Wendy Sewell.

In 1973, the 32-year-old was sexually assaulted and killed in Bakewell Cemetery in the Peak District.

Derbyshire police concluded the legal secretary was beaten with a pickaxe handle.

Stephen Downing, then 17, was convicted of her murder but was cleared after 27 years in jail. Nobody else has been charged with the killing.

Mr Clark, who the Daily Star Sunday revealed is looking at 17 more possible victims of Peter Sutcliffe, says the report is a vital breakthrough.

He said: "It was believed this report had been lost or destroyed over the years.

"However, it seems its conclusions had been ignored in the original trial and it had then gathered dust for decades.

"I managed to get hold of a copy and couldn't believe it when I read the pathologist's observations.

"He states that Wendy Sewell had sustained massive bruising to her neck and Adam's Apple. "This is consistent with being garrotted. She was then hit about the head with a heavy object. "It is a classic mode of attack used by the Yorkshire Ripper."

Home Office pathologist Alan Usher wrote: "The larynx hyoid bone...showed a massive ecchymoses (bruise)."

The report also reveals Wendy suffered deep bruising to the muscles at the back of her neck.

This is consistent with being forcibly grabbed from behind with a ligature.

Chris, who served with Norfolk Police, added: "Nowadays, the evidence of strangulation would not be missed."

The pathologist's evidence was not presented to the judge or jury at the 1974 trial of Downing or his appeals.

Downing, who had a reading age of 11, had made a false confession to murder.

Mr Clark said the strangulation, added to the frenzied and sexual nature of the murder, bore the hallmarks of the Ripper killings.

Don Hale, the local newspaper reporter whose campaign helped free Downing in 2002, said: "The evidence is compelling.

"It should be investigated in relation to the Yorkshire Ripper. The patterns of killing are almost identical."

One of Sutcliffe's victims, civil servant Marguerite Walls, 47, was stunned with a hammer and strangled with a rope in Leeds on August 20, 1980.

He also used a ligature to try to murder Dr Upadhya Bandara, then 34, in Leeds in 1980. She survived.

Mr Clark will pass the evidence to Her Majesty's Inspectorate of Constabulary, which assesses police forces. He hopes they will order a probe into the Derbyshire police inquiry that will spark new leads.

However, Derbyshire police are unwilling to reopen the case. The force told the Daily Star Sunday: "From a police perspective the case is now closed. All possible lines of enquiry were exhausted during the re-investigation."

The Ripper, now 67, is serving 20 life sentences in Broadmoor Hospital, Berkshire.

THE THIRTEEN KILLED BY SUTCLIFFE

Wilma McCann, 28; Oct 1975
Emily Jackson, 42; Jan 1976

Bakewell 1973 Stephen Downing; Carol Wilkinson Bradford 1977 Anthony Steele.

'I have recently acquired a copy of the pathologist report on the Wendy Sewell case and it is quite clear to me that the Home Office Pathologist Alan Usher in the company of 3 senior Derbyshire detectives found evidence at the post-mortem of Wendy Sewell on the 15th of September 1973 that asphyxiation pressure in the form of a ligature had been applied to her neck before being struck a number of blows to her head. It is also evident that Alan Usher found injuries to Wendy Sewell which resulted from kicking. I also conclude that there is evidence in his report to show that Wendy was dragged from the initial attack site to where she was subsequently found.

'It is my understanding that the contents of this part of the report in respect to asphyxiation were withheld and never put forward in evidence at Mr Downing's Trial, his subsequent first appeal, his second appeal or within Operation Noble in 2002 or [has] the existence of [this part of the report been] admitted by Derbyshire Constabulary who Refused my Freedom of Information Request during July 2013.

'As to the ramifications that have come to the fore – Conspiracy to Pervert the Course of Justice, Perjury and Malfeasance and Gross Misconduct against certain individuals and Derbyshire Constabulary, I am seeking your advice as to where this finding and material should be presented to. Whether it be to The Home Office Minister, Her Majesty's Chief Inspectorate of Constabulary, The Independent Police Complaints Commission or The Crown Prosecution Service.

Yours sincerely, Chris Clark (Mr).'

While the contents of this email were acknowledged, Chris was informed that Mr McLoughlin could only deal with his constituent's complaints. Nevertheless, Chris's findings were soon covered in the national press and both of us continued to contact the authorities.

The BBC, 15 January 2014:

'Wendy Sewell murder: pathology report contradicts conviction'

'A retired police officer has reported Derbyshire Police to the Home Office over claims they withheld evidence in a 1973 murder case. Bakewell man Stephen Downing was convicted in 1974 for killing Wendy Sewell but that was overturned in 2002. Chris Clark said he has uncovered a crucial pathology report showing she was strangled, which was never told to the jury.

'The Home Office said it would send any new criminal evidence to the police. Evidence of police misconduct would be referred to the Independent Police Complaints Commission, the Home Office added. Derbyshire police said the case was closed after a reinvestigation in 2002. Mr Clark, a retired Norfolk police officer, said he has sent his findings to the Home Office after obtaining the original pathology report last month. He said he believed the report

Pictures: STUART WILDE

TRAGEDY: Beaten and strangled Wendy Sewell, right, was found by Stephen Downing, then 17, left and below today

Murder evidence 'buried'

By Eugene Henderson

CRUCIAL evidence which could have prevented the longest miscarriage of justice in British history was "buried", according to a former police officer.

Chris Clark believes details of the autopsy carried out on "Bakewell Tart" murder victim Wendy Sewell were hidden to help convict a teenager of the killing more than 40 years ago.

He found "hidden" details of the post mortem report while looking into killings he believes may be linked to Yorkshire Ripper Peter Sutcliffe.

Stephen Downing, then a 17-year-old with learning difficulties, spent 27 years in jail be-

fore his conviction was quashed. He was arrested on September 12, 1973, after he found legal secretary Wendy Sewell covered in blood among graves at Bakewell Cemetery in Derbyshire.

Police questioned him for nine hours without a solicitor, before he signed a confession. Days later she died and workman Downing was charged with murder.

The trial jury heard Wendy Sewell, 32, who was cruelly dubbed the Bakewell Tart after it emerged she kept a diary of her lovers, was beaten with a pickaxe handle and sexually as-

saulted. Now details have emerged of the post-mortem exam by pathologist Professor Alan Usher which highlighted injuries to Wendy's throat and neck suggesting a ligature was used. He failed to include details of the injuries in his findings.

Mr Downing said last night he was not questioned about the neck injuries or the use of a ligature. "There was no mention of it back then," he said. "The police were out to get somebody and I was an easy target."

A police spokesman said he could not "confirm or deny" if the team that reinvestigated the murder knew of the report.

Sunday Express 12 January 2014.

showed Mrs Sewell had clear signs of being strangled. She was found battered in a Bakewell cemetery in 1973 and died in hospital two days later. Mr Downing admitted beating her with a pickaxe handle but later retracted that statement, only to be found guilty by a jury.

'Retired policeman Chris Clark said Peter Sutcliffe, the Yorkshire Ripper, could be connected with Wendy Sewell's murder: "I'm reporting the facts as I see them. The pathologist had evidence in his report that could have exonerated Stephen Downing," Mr Clark said. He said the pathologist's report showed bruising on her neck consistent with a "knotted ligature" used to garrotte her and a rash in her lungs and airways, possibly caused by strangulation. Mr Clark said none of this was used in Mr Downing's trial. He added the evidence may mean her death was linked to the Yorkshire Ripper, Peter Sutcliffe.

'Mr Downing was 17 at the time of Mrs Sewell's murder but was assessed as having a mental age of 11. His father Ray Downing and *Matlock Mercury* editor Don Hale campaigned for his release and in 2002 the Court of Appeal found his conviction unsafe because of "procedural reasons". Mr Hale said the pathology report directly conflicted with the evidence the police presented at the time and called for an independent investigation into the murder. "This information was available within two or three days of Mr Downing being arrested and it completely contradicts this so-called confession," he said. But Derbyshire police said the murder was reinvestigated following the quashing of the conviction and it considered the matter closed. "All possible lines of inquiry were exhausted during the reinvestigation. Twenty two people were ruled out of the enquiry but officers were unable to eliminate Stephen Downing as a suspect," a spokeswoman said. She added there was no evidence to suggest Peter Sutcliffe – the Yorkshire Ripper – was involved.'

On 7 March 2014, I wrote to The Home Office:

'Re: Murder Of Wendy Sewell. Dear Sir/ Madam. As part of an ongoing investigation of my case, I am informed that I am the only person who may seek copies of material that was presented in relation of my court case in 1973/4, and at subsequent appeals. I was further informed that following the investigation by Derbyshire Constabulary that a 95 year disclosure notice has been placed on the material rather than the customary 30 years. If this is true can you confirm it and explain to me why this is so? I am being assisted by a retired police officer, who informed me of the disclosure notices after he had contacted Theresa May, Home Secretary and was denied access to materials pertinent to the investigation. What I am looking for are copies of the four books of photographs produced by or on behalf of Derbyshire Constabulary that was [sic] entered at trial. My then acting legal firm, Messrs Woollcombe Beer Watts (now WBW Solicitors) have no documents in their archives, and I therefore seek to obtain them from you. I was never given copies of any photographs at the time of my trial or subsequent appeals although I did ask for them at the time of my trial and was informed that it would be too costly to produce copies for me. By the same token I never received a full set of documents, only my committal papers, the correspondence from my solicitors and notices of grants for legal aid. I therefore respectfully ask if I might be given copies of the photographs. Yours faithfully Stephen Downing.'

In April 2014, Chris and his wife Jeanne travelled by train from Durham to Chesterfield, and I took them to Bakewell to see Mum and Chrissie. After visiting the cemetery, where I showed them the geography and logistics of the case, we had a very enjoyable lunch at a local hostelry before their return back to Durham later that afternoon.

On 14 April 2014 Chris received the following from the CCRC:

'Dear Mr Clark, thank you for the Freedom of Information request you sent to the Commission via the *Whatdotheyknow* website. We spoke at some length on Friday, 11th April. I am writing to tell you that I did as we discussed and continued investigating whether or not the Commission had ever obtained the photographs about which you have asked in relation to its investigation of Mr Downing's murder conviction. I have established with a reasonably high degree of certainty that we did indeed obtain the relevant photographs from the police in 1997 when our review began.

'However, we returned all the original material that we obtained from the police on 7th February 2002. I can find no record of copies of the photographs having been made and retained by the Commission. As discussed on Friday, this accords with the fact that the Commission's referral of the Downing case to the Court of Appeal did not rely in any way on these photographs or on the post mortem examination with which they are associated. So, altogether this means that the Commission is not in possession of the information you have requested and therefore the question of whether or not we could disclose it to you in response to your request does not arise. Best of luck with your efforts to track them down. Regards Justin. Justin Hawkins Head of Communication Criminal Cases Review Commission.'

Chris also received this from the Home Office on 16 May 2014:

'Dear Mr Clark, Freedom of Information request - 31456 Thank you for your email of 17th April 2014, in which you request the post-mortem photographs of Wendy Sewell. Your request has been handled as a request for information under the Freedom of Information Act 2000. Your full request can be found in Annex A. I confirm that the Home Office does not hold any information on the post-mortem photographs of Wendy Sewell. Information Access Team, Home Office Ground Floor, Seacole Building 2 Marsham Street London SW1P 4DF.'

On 25 June 2014, in response to my appeal to the Home Office for the photographs, I received the following reply from The Crown Prosecution Service (CPS) and sent Chris a copy of their findings:

'Hi Chris this is to inform you that I have had a lengthy reply from the CPS to say that they will not be releasing the 4 books of photographs for the following reasons:

1) The photographs are too graphic for the surviving members of the family.
2) It would prejudice any chance of obtaining a conviction in the future.
3) It contravenes data protection act.
4) It is of no interest to the public.

'I don't know as there would be any member of the family seeing the photographs. Likewise I do not foresee the pictures being published, although they would lend weight to any published work in book form much as those of Jack the Ripper victims. It would also strengthen [the] description to the written text in helping the read[er] to understand what is said. It does give ways of appealing the decision, which is what I propose to do, as it would be in the public interest to find that a line has been drawn under the case in so much as my name being completely cleared. It would also mean that the police are not able to sit on their laurels and claim that they have in their opinion the only person they need to look for. In the event of the appeal failing then there is an avenue to appeal yet further. I feel that to really get anywhere it will need a solicitor at minimum to deal with the matter an[d] ideally a QC.

'I will send you a copy of the letter for your file. Wishing you both well. Stephen.'

In August 2014, my beloved mother died. Her funeral was on 15 September. Mother was given a beautiful send off by the vicar Tony Kournhoven. There were about twenty-five mourners in attendance and would have been more had they not been away on holiday. The funeral service was very respectful and we could not have asked for better. Mother did not have a will so on 17 September Chrissie and I went to see a solicitor in relation to probate.

I have always liked helping others and, in late 2014, I applied for a DBS (Disclosure and Barring service) check so I could undertake some voluntary work for the evacuation team (which rehouses people who have been evacuated in an emergency) at Derbyshire City Council. A few years ago, I had applied to work as a community responder with St John Ambulance and was honest with them about my conviction and explained that it had been cleared by the Court of Appeal. Although the DBS came back with no results, I didn't take up the work as I was only allowed to practise forty miles away in Derby, rather than locally, as they said local people would not want me in their homes. On 24 January 2015 I received the following response to my DBS application:

'After careful consideration the Chief Officer of Derbyshire Constabulary believes that this information ought to be disclosed because it indicates that there may be a risk of harm to those associated with Mr Downing. The application form indicates that the applicant has applied to work in the child and adult workforce and without knowledge of the information the registered body/proposed employer will be unable to complete an assessment of the risk of harm in relation to the specific duties of the position in which the applicant is to be employed. Therefore, on this occasion, the risk of harm to children and adults outweighs the impact of disclosure of the information on the private life of Mr Downing.'

On receipt of this, I sent an email to Chris:

'They have disclosed that I was convicted of murder and continue to be the only suspect for the offence and the Chief of Police feels that I am therefore high risk to adults and children. A few years ago I applied to be a Community Responder with St John Ambulance. I voluntary admitted to my conviction and it being quashed and my DBS came back as having no results. I still have the certificate somewhere and hope to use this as a way of showing double standards and believe that this is a ploy because of trying to obtain the photographs. I'm not unduly worried that the certificate has not been granted as it just means that I don't do voluntary work and others miss out. I think that it is fair to say that my blood is boiling though that they would stoop so low, but given that they are vindictive should not surprise me. All well this end and hope that the same for you. Regards Stephen.'

On 3 February 2015 I sent the following email to Mrs K.J. Bowman from the DBS Service Unit:

'Dear Mrs Bowman. Further to your correspondence I feel that I have to comment and say that it is very rich that I am expected to submit my defence within 14 days, but you can take 60 days and then delay issuing my DBS certificate with additional enquiries, thus giving you a further 60 days with the process back to the start.

'At this stage I am happy to submit self-defence. At the time of my appeal the Chief Officer was afforded every opportunity in which [to] submit his/her own findings and beliefs to the Court of Appeal, yet chose not to. The Court of Appeal found in my favour and quashed any conviction. In view of the above points the conviction never existed nor therefore did the charge and cannot therefore be used against me. The Chief Officer cannot have it both ways and must concede to my having no criminal history which can be used against me.

'If you look back in your records you will find that a certificate was issued, which I still have, although currently mislaid, for the purpose of my working with St John Ambulance and East Midland Ambulance Service as a First Responder, this is further proof that the Chief Officer is attempting to blacken my character. As the police are only too aware, I am not averse to taking matters before the courts (and winning) and will not hesitate [to] do so again to clear my name. Under the freedom of information act I would like you to send me copies of all information you hold against me. Yours sincerely Stephen Downing.'

On 4 March 2015, Chris and Jeanne again travelled down from Durham and stayed overnight in a local B&B as it was Chrissie's, Jeanne's and my joint birthday. Jeanne and I were born on the same day – 4 March 1956 – and so celebrated our 60th birthday together and we had a bit of a do.

In August 2015 Chris and I were featured in an ITV Midlands regional news programme which focused on Wendy Sewell's murder and my miscarriage of justice.

On Wednesday, 29 June 2016 I was featured in ITV Judge Robert Rinder's *True Crime* series, which explored my miscarriage of justice. Chris Clark and Don Hale also appeared in supporting roles.

After considerable training, I am now a fully-qualified counsellor in Clinical and Pastoral Counselling but am unable to practice without a DBS certificate. I can no longer seek other work as I am registered disabled due to osteoarthritis. I take daily medication and have a morphine-based transdermal patch applied weekly. Despite this, I have terrible pain and find it difficult to walk or stand for any length of time. Nevertheless, I will keep on fighting until the day I die in a bid to finally clear my name.

Stephen Downing July 2017.